THE GOOD GOLF GUIDE

BASIC GOLF RULES

This material previously appeared in *Improve Your Golf*.
This volume compiled by Paul Foston and Sally Hiller.

3297
Published in 1994 by Tiger Books International PLC, London
in association with CLB Publishing, Godalming, Surrey
© Eaglemoss Publications Ltd 1989, 1990, 1991, 1992
All rights reserved
Printed and bound in Hong Kong
ISBN 1-85501-410-6

THE GOOD GOLF GUIDE

BASIC GOLF RULES

TIGER BOOKS INTERNATIONAL
LONDON

CONTENTS

INTRODUCTION

All sports are governed by rules, and golf is no different, but what distinguishes golf from other games is their number and complexity. With so many rules it is impossible to know them all, and to make things even more difficult, each year the Royal and Ancient update or add rules to cover the ever-increasing eventualities that occur during a round of golf. Being aware of these rules is vital, because to ignore them can lead to disqualification. Whilst the majority of the rules do penalise you, there are many that can help. Knowing and understanding the rules can only lead to a more enjoyable round, whilst at the same time helping you to lower your scores.

Basic Rules of Golf covers a wide variety of situations that you are bound to encounter, and one or two that you may not have thought of. To find out more about the rules you can contact the Royal and Ancient, who will provide you with a complete, up-to-date rulebook.

Remember not to ground your club in a bunker. It's all too easy to forget this rule and use your normal pre-shot routine – but if you ground the club you are penalised 2 strokes in strokeplay and lose the hole in matchplay.

KNOWING THE RULES

Golf is no different from any other sport: you need rules and regulations so that it can be a fair game for all to enjoy. If you are a newcomer to the sport this section will be of interest as it will enable you to familiarise yourself with certain golfing terminology. Knowing the rules and how to use them can only make you become a more competent player.

Be careful about the flagstick on the greens. If your ball hits it – whether or not you have it attended – you suffer a 2 stroke penalty in strokeplay or lose the hole in matchplay.

Introducing the rules

**The rules of golf are there to guide you, whatever situation you find yourself in.
You get much more from the game if you know how to apply them properly.**

Golf began as one of the most straightforward of all games; it is now governed by the most complicated set of rules of any sport. Even those who make their living by playing the game – the tournament pros – often call for a ruling from an official when they are in doubt as to how to continue.

The most famous of modern British commentators on the game, Henry Longhurst, always maintained that the essential rules could be written on a postcard and the rest discarded, to everyone's advantage. But the detail of the rules means you can find guidance in any golfing situation, however unusual.

The rules are complex because those who make them have to legislate for a game played over vast areas of widely varying land, in all parts of the world. As soon as you start to play golf, you become aware that a long list of bizarre situations can arise – on almost all of which the rules can help you.

WHO MAKES THE RULES?

The two bodies responsible for the rules and their interpretation are the Royal and Ancient Golf Club of St Andrews (R and A) and the United States Golf Association (USGA). The USGA controls golf in North America. The R and A administers the rest of the golfing world – over 60 nations are affiliated to it.

You must come to terms with the rules if you are to play on the golf course. The code states that players may not agree to ignore a rule or a local rule or any penalty incurred. If you do disregard a rule, you are disqualified, under Rule 1-3, whether in strokeplay or matchplay.

You can refer any queries or disputes about the rules to the Rules Committee of the R and A. But they must be submitted through a club or competition secretary – individual requests would swamp an already over-worked body.

COURTESY ON THE COURSE

Golf etiquette is based on common sense and consideration for others.

Slow play is one of the bugbears of modern golf – many offences against etiquette are usually involved. For instance, if you are looking for a ball, you should call through any match waiting behind you without delay. Once you have done so, you should not continue play until the players called through are out of range.

Twoball matches have precedence over three and fourball matches and are entitled to pass them. Any match playing a whole round can pass through a match playing a shorter round. If you are a single player, you have no standing on the course and must give way to a match of any kind.

If you lose a clear hole on the match in front of you, you have lost your place on the course and should invite any following match to pass.

Rules about dress on the course are nothing to do with the etiquette of golf. Where they exist, they are rules of the club concerned, and your complaints – or congratulations – should be directed accordingly.

▲ Use a pitch-mark remover to tease the turf back up after your ball has landed on the green. And once you've completed the hole, don't lean on your putter while you take the ball out.

◄ It is an essential part of etiquette to protect the course – always replace divots on the fairway.

Etiquette:
Questions and Answers

Slow play

Q Last Saturday some friends and I were playing a fourball over 9 holes. We had a drink afterwards and, when the match behind reached the clubhouse, the players were clearly annoyed that we hadn't let them overtake us. They claimed that they had precedence over us because they were playing a full round. But, apart from the fact that we were being delayed by the slow match ahead of us, how could we have known that they were playing a full round?

A Many points of etiquette revolve around slow play. While it's irritating to be chivvied by a match following you, it is correct that a full-round match takes precedence over anyone playing a shorter round – even if the delay is not your fault.

As a general rule, be aware of players behind you and, if there's a bottleneck, let them know why they are being delayed. It is impossible to know whether the match behind is playing more holes than you are without asking – which is why communicating with other players is so important.

Raking bunkers

Q My opponent played from a bunker and put his ball on to the green. I then fluffed my chip from beside the bunker, which meant that my ball rolled back into the sand. When I went to play it, I found that my opponent had failed to rake the bunker, although a rake was provided, and my ball had rolled into a deep heel-mark he had made.

Section 1 of the Rules of Golf states that, before leaving a bunker, a player should carefully fill up and smooth over any holes and footprints he has made. Could I therefore have claimed the hole from my opponent in matchplay?

A No. The section on Etiquette in the Rules of Golf is a preliminary to the Rules themselves – you'll find that Rule 1 in fact comes nine pages later in the R and A approved booklet.

The section on Etiquette is highly important: note how it is placed at the beginning rather than as an appendix to the Rules. But it is a guide to how players should behave on the course, not part of the Rules of the game. Notice how this section suggests that you 'should' or 'should not' do things, while the Rules direct that you 'shall' or 'shall not' do things.

Your opponent's failure to repair the bunker was deplorable, but did not break a Rule of Golf. It is certainly not the way to win friends! Any prolonged disregard of the code of etiquette should be dealt with firmly by the Committee of the club.

Leaning on putters

Q I've seen pros on TV lean on putters when taking their ball out of the hole. Should they?

A No. Although copying the stars is excellent for improving your game, never follow their example in this area.

Noise factor
Remember that noise is distracting and puts off other players. Apart from not talking when someone's about to play a ball, never take personal stereos, radios or portable telephones on the course or any other devices that might annoy.

Parts of the course

**You may feel that you know all about the different sections of a
golf course. As far as the rules are concerned,
there are four areas and you need to be very clear in your mind
about the distinctions.**

Many players immediately think of the fairway as one of the major areas of the course. But the Rules of Golf do not use the word, preferring to deal in terms such as 'closely mown areas'. There are good reasons for this – for example, the rules have to cover par-3 holes, where fairways do not normally exist.

The four areas of a golf course each have their own rules. In the order you come across them, these areas are the Teeing Ground, Through the Green, Hazards and the Putting Green.

THE TEEING GROUND

The teeing ground on a particular hole varies from day to day. It is not all of what most players call 'the tee', but a rectangle which is always two club lengths in depth. Its width varies, because it is defined by the outside limits of the two tee-markers positioned by the greenkeeper.

You must play your ball from within this rectangle. It is up to you whether or not you place it on a tee-peg. As long as your ball is correctly positioned, you may stand outside the teeing ground to play it. However, you must not move either of the markers to give yourself a clear swing.

You are penalized if you mistakenly play from outside the teeing ground. In matchplay, your opponent may make you play again if he wishes – but he will probably be content to let the shot stand if you hit a bad one! There is no other penalty.

In strokeplay, you are penalized two shots and then have to play from the proper place. Strokes played from the wrong place do not count. You must put your mistake right before you tee off on the next hole – or leave the 18th green if the error occurs there – otherwise you are disqualified.

THROUGH THE GREEN

This is the whole area of the golf course except the teeing ground of the hole being played, the putting green of the hole being played and all hazards.

The term 'through the green' dates from well back in time. Remember that it embraces all of the course, because this means that relief (permission to move the ball) given on the fairway is generally also available in the rough. For example, you can claim the same relief from casual water whether you are in the middle of the fairway or deep in the rough.

HAZARDS

There are two kinds of hazards: bunkers and water hazards. The

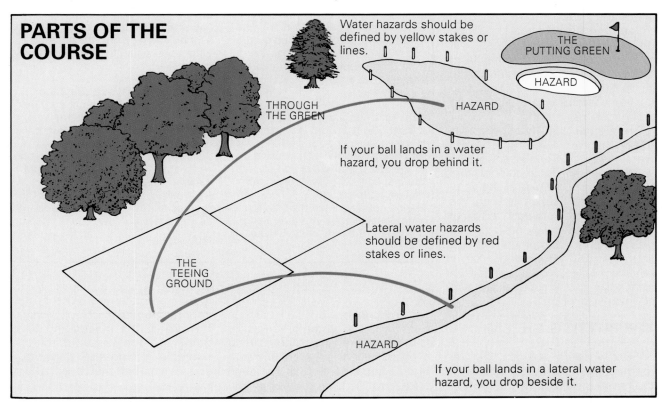

PARTS OF THE COURSE

Water hazards should be defined by yellow stakes or lines.

THE PUTTING GREEN

HAZARD

THROUGH THE GREEN

HAZARD

HAZARD

If your ball lands in a water hazard, you drop behind it.

THE TEEING GROUND

Lateral water hazards should be defined by red stakes or lines.

HAZARD

If your ball lands in a lateral water hazard, you drop beside it.

THE TEEING GROUND

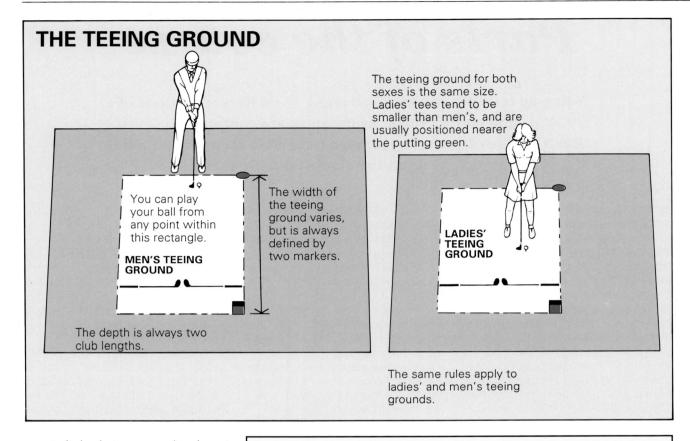

The teeing ground for both sexes is the same size. Ladies' tees tend to be smaller than men's, and are usually positioned nearer the putting green.

You can play your ball from any point within this rectangle.

MEN'S TEEING GROUND

The width of the teeing ground varies, but is always defined by two markers.

The depth is always two club lengths.

LADIES' TEEING GROUND

The same rules apply to ladies' and men's teeing grounds.

most vital rule to remember is not to ground your club in any kind of hazard. Grass-covered ground bordering or even within a bunker – some famous bunkers have islands of grass within them – is not part of the bunker.

Water hazards should be defined by yellow stakes or lines. These give you their limits and are themselves within the hazard.

Lateral water hazards should be defined by red stakes or lines. The rules about dropping your ball from these are slightly different, so the distinction is important. You drop *beside* a lateral water hazard and *behind* a water hazard.

Remember that water hazards need not necessarily contain water. Many on Spanish and Portuguese courses, for instance, contain water for only part of the year. But if they are defined as such, the rules apply. It's very easy to forget when perched desperately on the side of a dried-up stony ravine that you must not ground your club; if you do so, you lose the hole in matchplay and are penalized two shots in strokeplay.

THE PUTTING GREEN

This may seem obvious, but remember that the fringe (apron) of the green is not part of the green –

Course questions and answers

Wrong teeing ground

Q I played my tee shot in a match and drove out of bounds. We then realized that I had driven from the wrong teeing ground. Obviously my opponent did not wish to recall the stroke, but we were not certain where I should play my second ball from. Eventually, I teed my ball up on the correct teeing ground and drove from there, adding a two-stroke penalty. Was I right?

A As it was a matchplay, you should have lost the hole. However, you should have dropped a ball as near as possible to the spot from where you played the first ball – in other words, from the wrong teeing ground. You should not have *teed* the ball there, because it is not the teeing ground for the hole being played.

Toppling off the tee-peg

Q My ball fell off the tee-peg last week when I was in the course of my downswing, and I failed to hit it at all. My opponent said I could re-tee it without penalty as I had made no contact, but I thought I had to count what had already happened as an airshot, and play my second shot without re-teeing the ball. Was I correct?

A Yes. You have to count the stroke which you made at the ball, even though you did not hit it. It does not seem very fair, but at least you avoided a hernia! And because the ball is now in play, you cannot tee it up but must play it as it lies.

However, if the ball falls off its tee-peg on the tee or is knocked off as you *address* it, you can replace it on its tee without penalty.

though it may be cut almost as short.

If any part of your ball touches the green, it is on the green as far as the rules are concerned. Putting is often called 'a game within a game', because it calls for such different skills from the rest of the

game. It is also so as far as the rules are concerned, for there are important ones which apply only on the green. It's maddening to be penalized for a stupid mistake such as hitting the flagstick – you can avoid this if you know the rules.

Caddies

**You may think that the rules of golf only apply to
players, but be warned – caddies
are also subject to the rules and if your caddie breaks
one you take the penalty.**

Caddie duties are strictly de-fined in the rules and failure to observe these results in penalties.

When you use the services of a caddie, bear in mind that you are responsible for his actions. He acts on your behalf, so if he breaks any rules you will be penalized. For instance, if your caddie attends the flagstick and fails to remove it, so that your ball strikes it, you will suffer the penalty of loss of hole in matchplay or 2 strokes in strokeplay.

Equally, if your caddie moves an opponent's ball or touches it with your equipment, except while searching, you are penalized 1 stroke, just as if you had committed the offence yourself. He needs to know the rules thoroughly if he is not to incur unnecessary and costly penalties for you.

Your caddie may indicate the line of a putt when you are on the green, but he must not touch the line of that putt, even behind the hole.

The experienced caddie of John Daly – the 1991 USPGA Champion – almost cost his man 2 strokes. The caddie touched the green when he took out the stick after discussing a putt. Eventually the championship committee decided that the caddie had not touched the line of the putt when he rested the flagstick on the green, so that no penalty had been incurred by the player.

ONE CADDIE EACH

If your friends come out to watch you, remember that you are allowed only one caddie – it is too easy in this context to accept advice or help from more than one person.

In the 1991 English Amateur Championship, a player was penalized for taking advice from someone in the gallery when he already had a caddie. He would have been allowed to switch caddies during the round, but he was only allowed to use the services of one at a time.

▼ **In a friendly game it's common
for players to share a caddie. This
arrangement is allowed under the
rules. But, although it works well on
the tee, it can be difficult for the
caddie to work efficiently if the
players are on different sides of the
fairway.**

◄ ▲ Cleaning the ball and repairing your player's pitch marks are among the duties you can expect to perform if you act as a caddie for a friend.

Questions and answers

Caddie instruction

Q May a player's caddie swing a club and demonstrate how a shot should be played?

A Yes – provided there is no undue delay. The rules say that a player can always ask and obtain advice from his caddie.

Caddie and player?

Q I played in a big strokeplay competition this summer. One of the players with a late starting time caddied for his friend who was starting early with me. Later, the competitor who played with me went out and caddied for the player who had caddied for him. Surely this was not permitted by the rules?

A Yes it was. The rules forbid play on the course on the day of a competition, but they do not forbid you to spectate or act as a caddie. Nor do they forbid you to act as a caddie for someone else when you have completed your round.

Clumsy caddie

Q My opponent's caddie accidentally stepped on his ball. Was there a penalty?

A Yes – your opponent incurred a 1 stroke penalty, unless the caddie was searching for the ball, in which case there would be no penalty.

No permission

Q While we were looking for my ball, my caddie found a ball and lifted it for identification without my authority and without any announcement of his intention. It was indeed my ball.

A You incurred a penalty of 1 stroke. The ball should have been replaced. There was no additional penalty for failing to announce your intention to lift the ball for identification, since you were not in a position to do so in these circumstances.

On the rebound

Q My caddie had gone forward to act as a ball spotter. I hit him with my tee shot, and the ball went out of bounds. What was the ruling?

A In matchplay you lose the hole – just as if the ball had struck you or your equipment. In strokeplay you are penalized 2 strokes because the ball had hit your caddie, and as the ball was out of bounds, you also incur the penalty for that. You should then have played 5 off the tee.

Watery grave

Q A river runs in front of the 18th green at our course. I lifted my ball on the green and threw it to my caddie to be cleaned. Unfortunately she missed it and it disappeared into the river and could not be retrieved. I holed out with another ball. Presumably this was in order?

A No – the rules do not allow you to substitute another ball in these circumstances. You should have been penalized 2 strokes in strokeplay or lost the hole in matchplay.

On reflection

Q I asked my caddie to stand between me and the setting sun to lessen the glare in my face when I was playing a stroke. My opponent suggested this was against the rules. Was he right?

A Yes – it was the striking of ball rule, which states that a player must not accept protection from the elements when playing a stroke. Your caddie could have stood there while you sized up the shot, but he should have removed himself before you actually played it.

A PLAYER'S RESPONSIBILITY

There are a surprising number of things that the golfer must consider before even hitting the ball. For example, you must check your equipment carefully, make sure your golf balls are legal, ensure your card is marked correctly and signed by both parties. It is surprising how often tournament players are disqualified for such lapses, so make sure this doesn't happen to you.

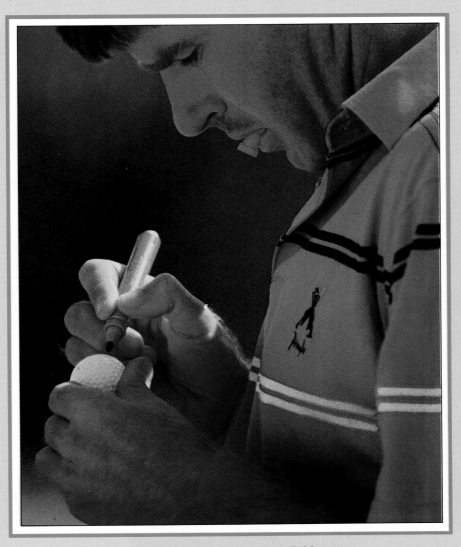

Professionals such as Nick Faldo recognise the importance of marking their golf balls. It's risky to rely on the maker's name and number – a similar type of ball may turn up and cause confusion.

A player's responsibilities

When it comes to the rules of golf, ignorance is no excuse and the penalties can be harsh. Every player must know what his or her responsibilities are before playing.

Your first responsibility as a player is to know the rules of golf. You have no right to waive a rule of golf, even by agreement with your opponent in matchplay. Even the committee, which has wide powers within the club, may not waive a rule of golf.

Some of the most important responsibilities involve punctuality, knowing about how a contest is played and scored, and handicaps.

COMPETITIONS

Where the committee has determined starting times, your first duty is to arrive at that time. Early starters held up on the way to the course may think they can simply be slotted into a later starting time. In fact, the penalty for failure to make your starting time is disqualification.

In exceptional cases this penalty may be waived or modified. If you arrive on the tee ready to play not more than five minutes after your starting time, you may be penalized by the loss of the first hole in matchplay or 2 strokes in strokeplay. Never be complacent about your starting time – always double check.

It's your responsibility to know the conditions of a particular competition. Which tees are you playing from? Assuming it is not a matchplay competition, is it a straightforward strokeplay or a Stableford competition? If it is Stableford, is it to be played off full handicap or seven-eighths?

The conditions for a particular competition are on the entry sheet or draw sheet in the clubhouse. It's up to you to check them.

HANDICAPS

Many disqualifications in contests result from failure to observe the rules about handicaps. In the vast majority of cases there is no intention to cheat, but the penalty stands.

In matchplay, you and your opponent should exchange details of your handicaps at the outset. If you begin a match having declared too high a handicap you are disqualified unless the number of strokes you give or receive is unaffected by the error.

When you give or receive three-quarters of the difference in handicap, the fractions can mean that one stroke too many on your handicap doesn't affect the number of strokes given or received.

If you declare a handicap which is too low, you will be held to this declared handicap. The general principle is that you can't claim shots retrospectively. If your opponent takes a stroke to which he is not entitled and you discover this later in the match, the result of that hole stands provided you had given each other the correct information about handicaps before the match began. It is up to you to know the holes at which shots should be given.

In strokeplay you must record

◄ **Record the score after every hole. In a competition, make sure you've checked beforehand what type of contest it is, and what handicap you are playing off.**

STABLEFORD SCORECARD

In Stableford scoring you receive 1 point for a bogey (one over par), 2 for a par, 3 for a birdie (one under par) and 4 for an eagle (two under par). The advantage of this system is that you can have one or two bad holes without wrecking your card.

You usually multiply your handicap by seven-eighths to work out how many strokes you receive for a round.

In this case player P Anderson has a handicap of 16 and so receives 14 strokes, one on each of the 14 most difficult holes (ringed in grey) as indicated by the stroke index.

On the first hole Anderson scored 6. Less one for the stroke given on that hole makes five, a par worth 2 points. His totals are shown in the win/loss column.

Competition STABLEFORD

Player A P. ANDERSON

Player B

Handicaps	Strokes Received	DATE
16	14	/ /

TIME — A.M. / P.M.

TEE — MEDAL

Marker's Score	Hole	Yards (Medal Tees)	Metres (Medal Tees)	Yards (Forward Tees)	Par	Stroke Index	Player's Gross Score	Win + Loss − Half 0 Points
							'A' 'B'	
	1	497	454	460	5*	9		2
	2	391	358	379	4	5	6	2
	3	200	183	196	3	15	5	2
	4	339	310	332	4	11	4	1
	5	440	402	420	4	1	4	3
	6	406	371	384	4	7	8	−
	7	140	128	140	3	17	7	−
	8	515	471	508	5	3	3	2
	9	324	296	318	4	13	5	3
Total		3252	2973	3137	36	OUT	46	16

Marker's Score	Hole	Yards (Medal Tees)	Metres (Medal Tees)	Yards (Forward Tees)	Par	Stroke Index	Player's Gross Score	Win + Loss − Half 0 Points
							'A' 'B'	
	10	183	167	183	3	16	6	1
	11	396	362	391	4	8	5	2
	12	434	397	426	4	4	5	2
	13	486	444	479	5	12	5	3
	14	485	443	430	5	2	7	1
	15	328	300	318	4	14	5	2
	16	373	341	366	4	6	5	2
	17	170	155	160	3	18	4	1
	18	366	335	360	4	10	4	3
Total		3221	2944	3113	36	IN	46	.16
		3252	2973	3137	36	OUT	46	16
		6473	5917	6250	72	Total	92	32

PAR 72

Marker's Signature

Player's Signature

Computer Number

Holes Won				
Holes Lost		Handicap	16	
Par Result	up	down	Nett Score	

32 pts.

---

your correct handicap on your card before it's returned. If you record no handicap, or one higher than that to which you are entitled, you will be disqualified from any handicap competition.

The only exception is again a logical one. In a Bogey or Stableford competition which is off less than full handicaps, you may find the number of shots you receive is not affected by the higher handicap you have given yourself on the card. In this case you wouldn't be disqualified.

If you enter too low a handicap on your card, your score will stand as recorded – the only penalty is the one you've given yourself by playing off too low a handicap. You can put things right even after your round is completed in strokeplay, but once your card is handed in you have to live with whatever errors you have made.

The committee has powers to adjust handicaps beyond the straightforward arithmetic of medal scores. Any such adjustments are posted in the clubhouse. Remember, it's your responsibility to make yourself aware of them.

Questions and Answers

Q Last week I played in my second Stableford competition. The first one had been played off full handicaps. Through ignorance and failure to check the conditions of the competition, I'm afraid that I assumed this one would be, too.

After the card had been handed in, I found that this Stableford was actually being played off seven-eighths of handicap. Although I returned to the secretary within five minutes to try to correct my mistake, he told me I was too late.

You can imagine my surprise and relief when my companion's correct score – the score he should have had off seven-eighths of his handicap – was eventually published among the results. Am I right in assuming the secretary was merely being charitable to me as a newcomer to the game?

A Several important points emerge from this.

First, even the secretary – in the unlikely event that he'd feel charitable to someone putting him to so much trouble – wouldn't be allowed to break a rule of golf. The rules say you cannot alter the card after you have returned it to the committee. Your secretary has in fact followed the rules to the letter. The second point to note is that it was your companion's duty to check his own card before signing it and handing it in.

Finally, it was your duty as a marker to record the player's gross score on each hole, having checked it with him. Since you obviously did this correctly, your errors in allotting too many Stableford points did not invalidate the card. The secretary computed the correct Stableford points in each case, and did the addition for the correct total.

A player's responsibilities

As a golfer you must be aware of your responsibilities – these can be as diverse as marking the scorecard, instructing your caddie or deciding whether or not to play during a storm.

The incorrect marking and checking of cards leads to a great deal of disappointment. It is by far the most common cause of disqualification – many golfers have learnt from bitter experience to check a card carefully before handing it in.

The responsibility for returning an accurate card rests squarely on the player. It's up to you to make sure your marker corrects any omissions or errors before you hand in the card. Don't forget to sign your card, and make sure your marker has signed – forgetting the obvious is a common blunder.

As a marker, you should check the competitor's score with him and record it after each hole. Sign the card and hand it to him at the end of the round. If you make a mistake when entering a score, correct it clearly during the round. It's sensible to initial any amendments, though the rules don't insist on this. Once you have handed in your card, no alterations are permitted.

Remember, the crucial point is not whether the total score is correct but that the score for each hole is accurately recorded. You're disqualified if your marker has omitted a score for a hole or recorded one that's too low.

If your marker records too high a score, you have to accept it unless it's corrected before the card is handed in.

DISCONTINUING PLAY

In matchplay you and your opponent may agree to stop playing unless this delays the competition. In strokeplay it's normally up to the committee to suspend play. The one exception allows play to stop if there is danger from lightning. But you can also stop if you are seeking a decision from the committee on a doubtful point, or if there is some other good reason such as sudden illness.

In any of these cases, report your reason for suspending play to the committee as soon as you possibly can.

▼ A caddie is allowed to help you line up putts, but take care you don't seek advice from more than one person. Check that your caddie is aware of golf rules and regulations – if he makes a mistake, you receive the penalty.

MARKING ERRORS ON A SCORECARD

After a match it's important to check the scorecard carefully for errors. Some mistakes carry no penalty while others lead to disqualification. The card below contains several errors.

The player has not entered his handicap and has also forgotten to record his score for hole 18. Each of these omissions would cause his disqualification.

He would receive no penalties for adding the first nine holes incorrectly, recording the second nine in the wrong column and amending the scores for holes 11 and 12 without having them initialled. The player and the marker have also signed in the wrong places but neither would be penalized for their error.

Handicaps		Strokes Received		DATE	6/10/89
				TIME	A.M. / P.M.
				TEE	

Competition. KIRIN CUP (MEDAL)

Player A. M. GAYNOR

Player B.

Marker's Score	Hole	Yards (Medal Tees)	Metres (Medal Tees)	Yards (Forward Tees)	Par	Stroke Index	Player's Gross Score 'A'	'B'	Win + Loss – Half O Points
	1	497	454	460	5*	9	4		
	2	391	358	379	4	5	5		
	3	200	183	196	3	15	4		
	4	339	310	332	4	11	6		
	5	440	402	420	4	1	4		
	6	406	371	384	4	7	4		
	7	140	128	140	3	17	5		
	8	515	471	508	5	3	5		
	9	324	296	318	4	13	5		
Total		3252	2973	3137	36	OUT	41		

SSS—Medal (White) Tees 71
SSS—Forward (Yellow) Tees 70   PAR 72
*   Medal Tees—Par 5
      Forward Tee—Par 4

Marker's Signature ... M Gaynor

Player's Signature ... M Clarke

Computer Number

Marker's Score	Hole	Yards (Medal Tees)	Metres (Medal Tees)	Yards (Forward Tees)	Par	Stroke Index	Player's Gross Score 'A'	'B'	Win + Loss – Half O Points
	10	183	167	183	3	16	5		
	11	396	362	391	4	8	5 / 6	4	
	12	434	397	426	4	4	4 / 5	5	
	13	486	444	479	5	12	3		
	14	485	443	430	5*	2	5		
	15	328	300	318	4	14	5		
	16	373	341	366	4	6	3		
	17	170	155	160	3	18	4		
	18	366	335	360	4	10	3 / 9		
Total		3221	2944	3113	36	IN	41		
		3252	2973	3137	36	OUT	80		
		6473	5917	6250	72	Total	12		

Holes Won			Handicap	
Holes Lost			Nett Score	68
Par Result	up	down	Enter the player's GROSS score at each hole.	

If the committee suspends play when you are in the middle of playing a hole, you can complete it before stopping. You mustn't start again until the committee tells you to, though you can lift and clean your ball.

CADDIES

It's important to remember that your caddie is your responsibility. If he breaches any rules, you incur the penalty. Make sure he is aware of the appropriate rules if you are going to ask him to do such tasks as attend the flagstick and advise you on the line of putts.

You can change your caddie during a round, but you may have only one at any particular time. If two or three friends come out to support you in an important match, it's easy for more than one to start offering you advice. Choose one of them as your caddie, and warn the others against helping you in any way. The penalty for the breach of this rule is disqualification.

Questions and Answers

Lost card

Q Last week we played our Monthly Medal round in pouring rain. It was one of those days when there don't seem to be enough hands to control umbrella, waterproofs, clubs, trolley, card, pencil and so on.

As we left the 18th green I was horrified to find I had lost my playing partner's card. He hadn't kept a complete record of his scores as marker on my card. We prepared a duplicate card, agreed the scores on each hole, and signed it. Was this in order?

A Yes, this is quite all right. Similarly, if you think a sodden card is unreadable, you may copy it out on to a new one at the end of a round.

Checking the score

Q I am the competition secretary at my club. Last week, one marker hastily left the course at the end of his round – he was going on holiday and had a plane to catch. He had marked a winning card, but then disappeared without remembering to hand it to the player. Despite repeated phone calls, we were unable to contact the marker. What should we have done?

A The committee or its representative – you in this case – should make every effort to reach the marker. This you obviously did. You should then accept certification of the score by someone who witnessed the round. If the round was not played as a threeball and there were no caddies present, this may be impossible.

If no one else witnessed the round, the score should be accepted without written confirmation from the marker.

Golf balls – the rules

**Before beginning a match, check your golf balls carefully
– they must be regulation size and easily
identifiable. And to avoid penalty during play, know exactly
when you can clean or change your ball.**

Before a ball is used in competitive play, it must conform to the tests approved by the Royal and Ancient Golf Club (R and A) or the United States Golf Association.

Every manufacturer of golf balls could produce a ball that can fly further than the best of the current balls, but the rules would not permit its use.

It's possible to buy illegal balls because many manufacturers sell balls rejected by the R and A. These are clearly marked as rejects and are perfectly good to use when practising but *never* in a match. If you use an illegal ball – even innocently – you'll be disqualified.

Regulation of equipment, and balls in particular, is one of the reasons why golf courses that have been played for over a hundred years are still a challenge today.

Although the larger golf ball, with a diameter of 1.68in (4.3cm), is nearly always used these days, you may occasionally come across the smaller ball with a diameter of 1.62in (4.1cm).

Both sizes were used in British competitions during the 1970s and 1980s, but today both professional and amateur competitions require that players use the larger ball. This 1.68in ball must weigh 1.62oz (46g).

IDENTIFYING YOUR BALL

Inform your opponent or marker of the make and number of the ball you are playing before you start a round. You should also place your own identification mark on the ball. Dot or initial your ball with a permanent marker.

Marking is often ignored, but it's surprising how often balls of the same make and number surface during searches.

The responsibility for playing the proper ball rests with you alone. You may lift a ball to identify it as your own anywhere on the course, except in a hazard. If you ball lands in a bunker you may brush aside enough sand to identify the ball.

If you do lift your ball, you must first tell your opponent in match-play or your marker or a fellow competitor in strokeplay.

You may clean the ball only enough to identify it. Once you have confirmed that it's your ball, replace it exactly where it lay. Make sure that the other player is able to watch the whole procedure.

If you don't say what you're doing or you lift the ball to identify

▼ **Think twice before you lift a ball to clean it – you may fall foul of the rules. You can clean the ball before each putt or when taking relief from an unplayable lie.**

WHOSE BUNKER BALL?

Beware of breaking the rules if your ball lands in a bunker

You may carefully brush aside enough sand to identify the ball but you mustn't lift it or you incur a one-stroke penalty.

You may find you still can't tell whether it's your ball – in this case you can take the shot without penalty. If it wasn't your ball the other player may place his ball where it originally lay in the bunker.

it in a hazard, you incur a penalty of one stroke.

It may be impossible to make sure you are addressing your own ball in a bunker – in this case, you can make the shot without penalty.

If it's found that the ball belongs to another player he can place it where it originally lay.

UNFIT FOR PLAY

You may change your ball at any time *between* holes whatever its condition.

If it becomes unfit for play *during* a hole, you may lift and inspect it as long as you have told your fellow players.

A ball must be visibly cracked, chipped or out of shape to qualify as unfit – superficial scratches are not reason enough to replace a ball.

If everyone agrees that the ball was damaged during the play of the hole, you may place another ball on the same spot.

It's not unusual for certain types of ball to become unfit for play. Professional golfers who use balata balls which mark easily often use eight or more balls during a round.

CLEANING YOUR BALL

There's often confusion about when you are allowed to clean your ball. Remember, to avoid penalty, it's your responsibility to know the rules.

You *may* clean your ball before each putt when you are on the green.

Out of courtesy to your fellow players make sure that you don't overdo the cleaning – once is usually enough.

You may also clean your ball when you're taking relief from an unplayable lie.

You may *not* clean your ball if you are lifting it for identification, to determine if it is unfit for play, or if it's interfering with or helping play.

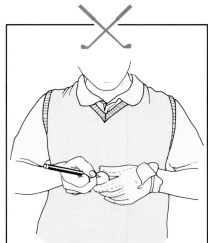

Marking your golf ball
It's important to mark your balls clearly before playing a round. A great deal of confusion is caused when identical balls appear during searches. And if you land in a bunker you can't lift a ball to identify it – you may end up playing the wrong one unless the balls are clearly marked.

Marking golf balls is a simple task – dot or initial them using a permanent marker.

Questions and Answers

Illegal ball

Q Quite unwittingly, I played a stroke with an illegal ball – one that was rejected by the R and A – in our medal competition. I substituted a correct ball as soon as my marker pointed out the error. What is the correct penalty?

A Disqualification is the penalty. If you use an illegal ball during a match, you are automatically disqualified.

To avoid an upset like this, it's essential that you check your balls carefully before playing.

Broken ball

Q When I was playing the other day with a solid ball, it split in two with part of it going out of bounds. I counted the shot, and played my next shot from where the biggest fragment lay. Was I correct?

A No, you shouldn't have continued with the shot. The stroke that broke the ball must be replayed without penalty. You should drop a ball as near as possible to the original spot.

Identifying your ball

**Whether you mark your ball with a pen or recognize
it in some other way, it's vital to
be able to identify it correctly. You are liable
for penalties if you play the wrong ball.**

It is entirely your responsibility to play the correct ball. If you are in any doubt as to whether a particular ball is yours, you should check it for yourself, whatever anyone else on the course has told you. The penalties for playing wrong balls are yours, not those of the golfer who misinformed you.

Everyone has played a wrong ball at some time. Nearly always this is through carelessness, which makes it more infuriating. Golf is enough of a challenge without incurring avoidable penalties. The penalties can be very severe: if you don't recognize your error in time, they can even lead to disqualification.

MARKING YOUR BALL

You must be able to identify your own ball with complete certainty. This means that you should put an identification mark of some kind on your ball – in fact the rules require you to.

Most players rely on the maker's name and number on the ball, confining their efforts to checking on the first tee that they are playing a different ball from those of their companions.

It's surprising how often you come across a ball of the same make and number when you are searching for your own. You should really have some additional mark to establish that it is your ball. Unless it's a brand new ball, it is likely to have some distinctive blemish which you can use.

▶ **Professionals such as Nick Faldo
recognize the importance of having
an easily identifiable mark on their
golf balls. It's risky to rely only on
the maker's name and number – a
similar type of ball may turn up and
cause confusion. It's your
responsibility to play the right ball,
so use an indelible pen to make an
identifiable mark.**

WHOSE BALL?

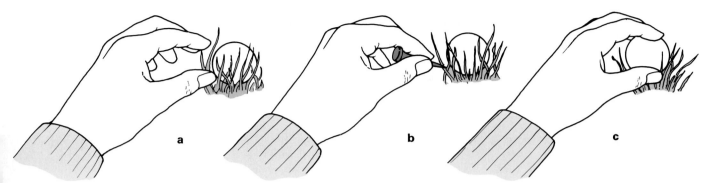

a

b

c

You can ease back the grass to identify your ball (a), but you mustn't improve the lie. If you're still not sure whether the ball is yours, you can lift it but you must announce your intentions and let the other players observe your actions.

Mark the ball's position (b), before you lift it (c). Clean the ball only enough to make sure it's yours, then replace it carefully.

There's no penalty for playing the wrong ball from a hazard – in this case, don't lift the ball.

PICKING UP THE BALL

Except in a hazard, you may lift a ball you think is yours to check it, and even clean it as far as it is necessary to identify it. There are two points to remember if you wish to do this.

First, you must announce your intentions to your opponent in matchplay, or your marker or a fellow competitor in strokeplay. Give that person the opportunity of observing what you do.

Second, as always when lifting a ball, you must remember to mark the position of your ball before you lift it. If you don't follow these guidelines you incur a penalty of 1 stroke.

In a hazard – any bunker or water hazard – there is no penalty for playing a wrong ball. Because of this, you may not lift your ball to identify it there.

The normal penalties for playing a wrong ball anywhere except in a hazard are loss of hole in matchplay and 2 strokes in strokeplay.

Questions and Answers: Ball identification

Lost ball

Q My opponent sliced his ball into trees to the right of a par-3 hole. After searching for about three minutes, we found a ball of the right make and number. He had not put an identification mark on his ball. As he was about to play, I found another ball of the same make and number. What should the decision have been?

A Normally when you find a ball of the correct name and number, you may assume it is the right one unless there are clear signs from its condition that it is not, or another ball of the same brand and number is found in the area. In your case, you would need to decide between you which of the two balls was the correct one.

If you found the second ball after your opponent had played, and decided between you that this was more likely to have been his ball, he would have lost the hole to you in matchplay. It is normally the player who is best qualified to identify his own ball in these situations, since he knows the condition of it and any marks it acquired in the course of play.

Rough justice

Q In our last monthly medal, I found my ball lying almost buried in the rough. Having announced my intention to my marker, I carefully turned the ball to check that it was mine, which it proved to be. I did not clean it in doing so, and I was very careful not to improve my lie.

I was surprised when my marker said that I should be penalized a stroke for doing this, and even more surprised when the committee upheld this decision. Were they correct?

A Yes – you touched the ball in a manner not provided for under the rules. Your mistake was not to mark your ball before touching it – in which case you could have done exactly what you did without penalty. You could even have picked up the ball to check that it was yours, provided that you returned it to exactly the same lie.

Ball in hazard

Q My opponent's ball came to rest in a dry ditch which was marked with red posts as a lateral water hazard. He marked the ball and turned it carefully to make sure that it was his before playing it. He did not improve the lie or clean the ball. Was this in order?

A No – you are not allowed to touch your ball in any hazard to identify it. Your opponent incurred a 1 stroke penalty for touching his ball on purpose. He need not have been so anxious to identify his ball, as he would have incurred no penalty for playing a wrong ball in a hazard.

Teeing your ball

**It pays to find out which tees you are to play from
before you start a game. Playing
from the wrong teeing areas makes you liable for
penalties that can easily be avoided.**

The teeing ground is a rectangular area defined by markers. You should make sure which tees you are to play from before you start – they're colour coded. These conditions are usually outlined on the entry sheet for strokeplay or Stableford competitions, and on the draw sheet for matchplay competitions.

You must not play from the area in front of the line between the markers, but you may play from anything up to two club lengths behind it.

PENALTIES

If you play from outside this area in strokeplay, you pick up a 2 stroke penalty. You are disqualified if you play a stroke from the next teeing ground without correcting your mistake. If you leave the last putting green without correcting your error you also face disqualification.

The penalties for carelessness are heavy. It's quite easy to go to the wrong tee on your own course from habit, when the competition tee may be in a different place from the usual one.

The penalty is less severe in matchplay. If you play from outside the teeing ground, your opponent may immediately require you to play a ball from within the correct teeing ground. Whether he chooses to do so depends on the result you achieve with the wrong stroke. He'll let the stroke stand if he thinks you're likely to improve on it with a stroke from the proper place.

PLACING THE BALL

You don't have to place the ball on a tee peg to start a hole. You can find a good lie on the grass, or knock up the turf – whatever suits you best. You can stand outside

▼ **The teeing ground is rectangular – defined by the outside limits of two markers on either side. The area is two club lengths long. You can tee up your ball from any part of the teeing ground – you can even stand outside it and play your shot. As long as the ball is within the limits of the teeing ground you aren't penalized.**

◄ Bear in mind that you must never move the teeing markers to help you play a shot. If you break this rule you lose one hole in matchplay and 2 strokes in strokeplay. Remember that you don't have to use a tee peg when preparing your shot (inset). You can simply knock up the turf slightly to give yourself a good lie.

the teeing ground to play your ball, provided that the ball itself is teed inside it. But you may not move a tee marker to help you play your shot. If you do, you are penalized one hole in matchplay or 2 strokes in strokeplay.

If your ball rolls off a tee peg or you knock it off at address before you begin the play of a hole, you can re-tee it without penalty – the ball is not in play at the time. But if you play an air shot and then re-address the ball and accidentally knock it off the tee peg, you are penalized 1 stroke. Even an air shot puts the ball in play. You must replace the ball and take a 1 stroke penalty.

Sometimes a ball rolls off the tee peg when you've started your swing and it is too late to stop and re-tee it. If a stroke is made at the ball in these circumstances, the stroke counts but there is no penalty – whether or not the ball is moving.

Questions and answers: Teeing your ball

Touching at address

Q In a recent match, my opponent put his shot from the teeing ground out of bounds. He teed up another ball, but in addressing it he touched the ball and it fell off the tee. He teed up the ball again and continued to play.

As he had begun play of the ball and this was in effect his third shot (because of the penalty he took for the out of bounds shot), should this not have counted as a shot as the ball was in play?

A No – a teed ball is not in play until a stroke has been made at it. He was in order to re-tee his ball.

Swing slip

Q I teed up towards the back of the teeing ground, but

slipped during my swing and barely moved the ball at all. As it was still within the teeing ground, could I have teed up again?

A No. The ball was in play after your first attempt.

Wrong course

Q After playing ten holes on the Old Course at Sunningdale, we stopped briefly for refreshments. When we started to play again, we played from a tee on the New Course by mistake. We realized our error before we finished the hole and returned to the 11th tee on the Old Course to complete the round. What penalty would we have incurred in strokeplay?

A It's an easy mistake to make. The penalty in strokeplay is 2 strokes. The strokes you played on

the wrong hole don't count.

Playing from the wrong tee

Q In our last monthly medal, I played from the wrong teeing ground and put the ball out of bounds. I then played another ball from within the correct teeing area. My marker thought I should be penalized 4 shots – 2 for playing from the wrong teeing ground and 2 for the ball which went out of bounds. Was he correct?

A No. You are penalized 2 shots for playing from outside the teeing ground, but this ball was then not in play. The fact that it came to rest out of bounds was irrelevant.

Looking for your ball

**There are specific guidelines to follow
when you lose your ball.
If you're aware of the rules, you can avoid
picking up needless penalties.**

Even the best golfers have to search for a ball sometimes. You are allowed five minutes to look for your ball. The five minutes start when the search for the ball begins – not when you hit it. That means when your side – you, your partner and your caddie – start the search, not when any spectators or opponents begin to look.

Many golfers are vague about time. It's up to you to police yourself – if you haven't timed the start of your search, you should accept the view of anyone who suggests that your time is up.

Most golfers don't use the full time limit to search for a ball in friendly matches. If the competition is important enough for you to spend time searching, make sure you call other matches through when you see them waiting.

NATURAL OBSTRUCTIONS

When looking for your ball anywhere on the course, you may touch or bend long grass, heather, bushes or other natural vegetation, but only enough to find your ball and identify it as yours. You must not improve the lie of your ball, the area of your swing or your line of play.

If you cannot be sure the ball is yours, you may lift it to identify it, provided that you replace it in exactly the same lie. According to the rules, you're not necessarily entitled to see your ball when playing a shot.

If you or any member of your side moves your ball other than to find or identify it, it costs you a penalty shot. But if the ball is moved

◀ **You are allowed to look for a lost ball for five minutes. If you can't find it, you must go back to where you hit the ball from and take a 1 stroke penalty.**

by a member of the other side, or a fellow competitor or his caddie in strokeplay, there is no penalty. You replace the ball and play on. This applies only to searching for a ball. Touching or moving an opponent's ball leads to a 1-stroke penalty at other times.

There is no penalty for playing a wrong ball in a hazard, so you don't have to be certain that a ball is yours before you play a shot.

If your ball is covered by loose impediments or sand in a hazard, you are allowed to remove enough of this material to help you see a part of your ball. If you remove more than necessary, you must replace the material until only a part of it is visible. If you move the ball in probing or raking like this, there is no penalty, provided that you replace the ball in the same position.

In a water hazard, the rules say that there must be 'reasonable evidence' that your ball has lodged in the hazard before you can presume that it has been lost there. For instance, if the hazard is surrounded by fairway and you can't see your ball on the grass, it is reasonable to assume that it has gone into the water.

▲ ► **If your ball is stuck in a tree, you can use your club to dislodge it and identify it as yours. If you can't free your ball, resign yourself to a 1 stroke penalty and take a drop two club lengths from the place where the ball is lodged.**

Questions and answers

Over the limit

Q What happens if a player goes on searching for a ball longer than the five minutes which the rules allow?

A Searching for the ball after the time allowed is pointless as, even if the ball is found, it is said to be lost after the five minute period. The player is also subject to a penalty for delaying play. In matchplay this is a loss of a hole while in strokeplay it's 2 strokes. You're liable to be disqualified for repeated offences.

Declaring a ball lost

Q My companion searched for his tee shot for two minutes, then declared it lost and went back to play another ball from the tee. Before he played, I found his first ball within the five minute period allowed. He thought that he had made the original ball a lost one by his declaration and by going back to the tee, and that he therefore had to play 3 from a tee. Was he correct?

A No. This is a common misunderstanding easy to make if you've watched similar occurrences in professional tournaments on television. When you have seen a professional having to play a second ball in this situation, it is because he has exhausted his five minute search period before abandoning the ball.

A player cannot make a ball lost by declaration. As the original ball was found within the five minute search period, it remained the ball in play. If the player had actually played another ball, or even dropped one other than on the tee, it would have become the ball in play.

Unplayable ball

Q Last summer in Spain my ball lodged in a palm tree. I was able to get near enough to it to identify it as my ball, but not to retrieve it. My companion thought my ball should be deemed lost as I could not retrieve it. Was he right?

A No – as the ball was identified, it was not lost. You could declare it unplayable and carry on under that rule. Players usually choose to drop within two club lengths of the ball – taking a 1-stroke penalty. In your case you are allowed a drop within two club lengths of the spot on the ground immediately beneath where your ball was lodged.

If you could see a ball in the tree but not identify it as yours, your ball would be deemed lost. You would be allowed to shake the tree, or even throw a club at the ball, in an attempt to dislodge and then identify it.

Hidden ball

Q My ball was almost invisible in a bunker because it was covered with leaves. I knew I was not allowed to move loose impediments in hazards, but don't the rules allow me to remove enough debris to see part of the ball? When I took my stance to play my shot I couldn't see any part of the ball. Could I have removed enough leaves to let me see the ball?

A No – the ball was not invisible in the bunker, because you could see it from one angle. You are not necessarily entitled to see the ball when playing a shot. If you thought the shot was impossible, you could have taken a drop within the bunker, under penalty of 1 shot.

Playing a provisional ball

**You can play a provisional ball if you think your
original ball is lost and you don't
want to delay play to look for it. But be sure to
follow the correct procedure.**

If you think that your ball may be
lost you should play a provisional
ball. The only exception is in a water
hazard or out of bounds.

You should tell your opponent in
matchplay, or your marker or fellow
competitor in strokeplay, that you
intend to play a provisional ball. Play
it before you or your partner looks
for the lost ball.

If you don't do this, your second
ball automatically becomes the
ball in play and the original ball is
assumed to be lost. So if you were
playing a second ball from the tee,
you will have played your third shot
because you take a 1 stroke penalty
for a lost ball.

You can continue to play strokes
with your provisional ball until you
reach the place where the original
ball is likely to be. If you play a
stroke from that place or any point
nearer the hole, the provisional ball
becomes the ball in play.

UNPLAYABLE LIES

If you play a provisional ball from
the tee then you find your original
ball in bounds but in an unplayable
position, you have three options.
You can find somewhere within two
club lengths to take a drop, or
choose a spot on the ball-to-target
line – but not nearer the hole. You
may also play your next shot from
where the last one was played –
adding a 2 shot penalty.

In this situation you're not allowed

to play a provisional because the
ball becomes dead as soon as you
found your original ball. You must
go back to the tee and play a third
ball, under penalty of stroke and
distance.

▼ **If a shot lands in dense
woodland, it saves time to play a
provisional ball before you search
for the lost original. Declare your
ball as provisional or it becomes the
ball in play.**

Who plays first?
There is sometimes confusion
over which partner plays a
provisional ball in foursomes. If
you play and think you may have
lost the ball or put it out of bounds,
it is your partner who plays the
provisional ball, because penalty
strokes do not affect the order of
play.

Questions and answers: provisional balls

Visible ball

Q My opponent was driving badly. Although his ball was clearly visible not far from the tee after a bad shot on the 4th, he hit a second ball, which he declared as a provisional, in an attempt 'to play himself into form'. Was this in order?

A No – there must be a reasonable possibility that the original ball is lost or out of bounds before a provisional is allowed. Your opponent's second ball would become not a provisional but the ball in play.

Permission to search

Q At our par-3 13th hole my opponent hit his tee shot into dense scrub. He then hit a provisional ball, which came to rest very near the hole.

He walked past the area where his first ball lay, saying that he wouldn't look for it – he was happy to see it lost. Would it have been in order for me to search for his first ball, even though he did not wish to do so?

A Yes. But if your opponent walked on to the green and played a stroke at the provisional ball before you found the first one, it would become the ball in play. This is because he had played from nearer the hole than the spot where the original ball lay.

In matchplay you could recall the stroke if he had played out of turn, but that would not change the status of the original ball, which becomes lost as soon as the provisional is played from nearer the hole.

If you found the original ball before he played any further stroke, it would become the ball in play. The provisional would be a dead ball.

Search order

Q I hit my ball into rough on the right of the fairway and my opponent hit his into rough on the left. We both had caddies. My opponent's caddie went to look for his ball, while everyone else moved to look for mine.

My opponent shouted to his caddie that he should not begin to search until everyone else was ready to help. Was this in order?

A Yes – you don't search at the same time as your opponent.

Time allowed

Q I hit both my original ball and my provisional ball into deep rough.

Was I allowed a total time of five minutes to search for both, or five minutes for the first and then another five minutes for the provisional?

A If the two balls are so close together that you are searching for both of them at once, you are allowed only a total of five minutes. Otherwise you are allowed five minutes for each ball.

Unannounced ball

Q I put my tee shot deep into the woods. Deciding that my second ball should be the ball in play, I did not announce it as a provisional. Could I still have had a quick look for my original ball, which was new?

A Yes, but you cannot play the original ball if you find it – and you must not unduly delay play.

TAKING A DROP

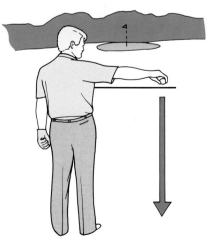

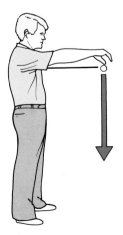

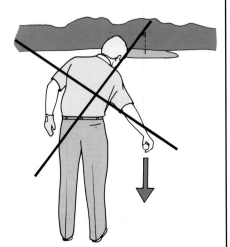

If you have to take a drop, you must drop the ball close to the place where it originally lay – but no nearer the hole.

To drop properly, stand straight and hold your arm at shoulder height. You can then drop the ball. You may extend your arm directly in front of you or to the side, whichever you prefer.

You may see a player lowering an arm and dropping the ball gently on a good lie, but while this may be acceptable in a friendly game it is illegal in competitions.

Slow play

**Every golfer has experienced the frustration of being
held up on the course by a slow group ahead.
The rules penalize players for undue delay but it is a
difficult term to define.**

If you know you're holding up the group behind you, it's courteous to allow them to play ahead of you so they can finish their round at a faster pace.

Slow play is one of the bugbears of modern golf. In this area the professional tour does not set a good example. Although many professionals like Ian Woosnam and Lanny Wadkins are fast players, they are victims of the general pace of the course.

DIFFICULT DEFINITION

The rules state that each player must play without undue delay. This is vague because it is difficult for authorities to define the term undue delay more precisely. The European Tour has issued guidelines to players on the maximum reasonable time that should be spent over a stroke and some fines have been imposed.

It is difficult to be exact about slow play in the case of the professional tour, since factors such as the size of the crowd following a particular match and the efficiency of crowd marshalling are outside the control of the players.

THE AMATEUR GAME

Amateur golf, however, does not suffer these difficulties. It is up to the committee of individual clubs to ensure that play proceeds at a reasonable pace on their courses, and particularly in their competitions. You should be ready to play when your turn comes, rather than thinking about club selection and assessing the shot at that stage.

The rules also remind you that you should not delay play after you've finished a hole and before you start the next. It is much easier to detect unwarranted slowness here. Use common sense in recording scores if you are in a strokeplay competition, so that you are not standing marking a card when you should be teeing your ball to drive.

Never mark cards on the green of the hole just completed. And leave your clubs near to the next tee or the path to it rather than in front of the green, where they can delay the group behind you.

The penalties for undue delay are quite clear. In matchplay you lose the hole. In strokeplay you lose 2 shots, with a penalty of disqualification for repeated offences. If you delay play between holes, the rules say that you are delaying play of the next hole and the penalty applies to that hole.

▲ **Even top professionals like Payne Stewart are victims of slow play** **and are forced to spend frustrating periods waiting between holes.**

Questions and answers

Current concern

Q A stream on our course is marked as a water hazard, but it is sometimes possible to play from it. My opponent found that his ball was moving slowly down the stream with the current. He waited until it moved to a shallow stretch and then played it out of the hazard successfully. Did he break any rule?

A Yes he did. He was allowed to play out of the water hazard, provided that he did not ground his club or touch the water in taking his stance. But in waiting for the ball to move to a more favourable place, he unduly delayed play. He should have lost the hole in matchplay or have been penalized 2 strokes in strokeplay.

On the edge

Q My ball was overhanging the edge of the hole after I had putted. I walked up to it, and then waited 40 seconds, at the end of which the ball dropped into the hole. Surely there was no penalty for this?

A Yes there was. The rules allow you only ten seconds to see whether your ball drops into a hole. After that, the ball is deemed at rest. When your ball fell after 40 seconds, you were deemed to have holed out with your last stroke, but had to add a penalty of one stroke. Sam Torrance was penalized when he waited more than ten seconds for his ball to drop into the hole during the 1990 English Open.

Uncertain lie

Q We were not sure whether my second shot was out of bounds or in a water hazard. It was almost 200yd (182m) ahead of us. In view of the rule which entitles a player to find out from an opponent the number of strokes he has taken, my opponent wished to go forward to find where my ball was before he played. Was he allowed to do so?

A No – he would have been unduly delaying play. He may find out where the ball is only if he can do so without unduly delaying play.

Forgotten club

Q I arrived at a green to find that I had left my putter on the tee, over 500yd (457m) away. If I had returned to the tee and delayed play would I have been subject to penalty?

A Yes – you would have lost the hole in matchplay and been penalized 2 strokes in strokeplay.

Long search

Q What happens if a player searches for a ball for longer than the five minutes in the rules?

A He is subject to the penalties for undue delay – loss of the hole in matchplay and 2 strokes in strokeplay.

BALL PROBLEMS

What do you do if your ball is plugged, struck out of bounds, unplayable, or up against a wall? Knowledge of the rules becomes essential if you are to play 18 holes without infringing them. There are so many rules that it is impossible to know them all by heart, but you should make sure you familiarise yourself with the more common ones.

Staying unruffled is vital to the Lyle approach. When faced with a daunting shot, he never worries about the stroke until he has arrived at his ball and seen exactly how it lies.

Playing a plugged ball

**On most areas of the golf course you can claim
relief if you find that your
ball is plugged – embedded in its own pitch mark.
Watch out for the exceptions.**

If you find that your ball is plug-ged in any closely mown area through the green you may lift, clean and drop it as near as possible to the spot where it lay but not nearer the hole.

Remember that through the green is the whole area of the course except the teeing ground and putting green of the hole you are playing and all the hazards.

A closely mown area is any area of the course that is mown to fair-way height or less. It includes areas such as paths cut through the rough, provided they are cut as low as the fairways. The grass faces of bunkers are not closely mown areas unless they are cut to the same height as the fairways.

If your ball moves out of its pitch mark, but then screws back into it in a closely mown area, it is counted as plugged for the purposes of this rule, and you may claim relief. If you drop a ball in a soft area of fairway and it plugs there, you are entitled to drop it again. Let your opponent or marker watch you do this.

▶ **You can take relief from a plugged ball only through the green in a closely mown area. This means the grass must be mown to fairway height or less – from semi-rough that's higher than the fairway grass you have to play the ball as it is or take a penalty.**

pro tip

Winter rules
In many cases of plugged balls, winter rules may be in operation. These allow you to lift, clean and place the ball on fairways and aprons, usually within 6in (15cm). The advantage is that you can choose your own lie instead of taking an unreliable drop.

Winter rules are local rules which may vary from club to club, so check before you play.

IN THE ROUGH

What happens if you find your ball plugged in the rough? There is no relief without penalty. You can always declare your ball unplayable and take a 1 shot penalty. You can then play the next stroke as near as possible to the original spot or take a drop within two club lengths of the place where the ball lay – but not nearer the hole. Or you could take a drop behind where the ball lay on the ball-to-target line.

Relief under penalty is often a better choice than making a savage attempt to move a plugged ball. But the decision is yours.

CLAIMING RELIEF

There are a few situations where you may be able to claim relief for a plugged ball in the rough. Casual water may occur anywhere on the course, as may ground under repair. If your ball is plugged in either of these, you may lift it and take relief without penalty anywhere through the green.

Be careful how you define casual water. Soft, mushy earth is not casual water unless water is visible on the surface after you have taken your stance. But water overflowing from a water hazard is casual water once it extends beyond the boundary of the hazard.

If your ball plugs in a molehill or a hole made by a burrowing animal, you can always claim relief without penalty wherever it occurs on the course.

Questions and answers: plugged balls

Is it plugged?

Q It isn't always easy to be certain whether a ball in a small depression on the fairway is embedded in its own pitch mark or not. I had such an instance in our last medal. I played the ball as it lay to avoid a possible penalty for touching my ball when this was not allowed. Could I have lifted my ball to see whether it was plugged in its own pitch mark?

A Yes. Even with a rule book as comprehensive as the one which governs golf, there are some points not clearly covered. This is one of them. But the rules do state that decisions in such cases should be made 'in accordance with equity'.

You could lift your ball without penalty in this situation, provided as always that you announced your intention to your opponent in matchplay or your marker or a fellow competitor in strokeplay.

If you find the ball is embedded in the ground in its own pitch mark, you take relief. If not, you replace it where it was, letting the person you informed of your intention watch you.

Topped shot

Q Playing from the downslope of a dip in the fairway, I topped the ball savagely with a wood. The ball never lifted off the ground, and finished plugged in the steep bank in front of me. As the bank was part of the fairway, I extracted the ball and dropped it no nearer the hole but as near as possible to the spot where it had plugged. Was this correct?

A No – the rule says that relief is allowed if the ball is embedded in its own pitch mark. The word pitch implies that the ball has become airborne.

Molehill relief

Q On a par 3 hole, my ball plugged in the rough wide of the green. It was in a molehill which had been swept flat by the green staff. I claimed relief from the molehill without penalty. Was I correct?

A No – when a molehill has been swept flat, it becomes just an irregularity of surface and there is no relief without penalty.

Casual water

Q My ball plugged deeply in short rough. No casual water could be seen on the surface when I took my stance, but the pitch mark was filled with water around the ball. Could I have taken this as evidence of casual water and dropped without penalty?

A Yes, in these circumstances you could claim relief.

ROUGH PLUG

If you're plugged in the rough you can declare the ball unplayable and take relief under penalty of one shot. This is often a safer option than playing the ball where it lies, but the choice is yours.

FAIRWAY PLUG

You can lift, clean and drop your ball if it's plugged on the fairway. Drop it as near as possible but not nearer the hole – if the ground is soft and it plugs again, you can drop a second time.

Improving your lie

**Like it or not, you play the ball from where it stopped.
But there are some exceptions
where you can take relief without a penalty.
It pays to be aware of them.**

Y ou usually play the ball as it lies, accepting bad luck as part of the game. If you find yourself in a divot mark or other unpleasant lie in mid fairway, you have to play the ball as it lies. You may feel this is harsh but it is part of the rules.

EXCEPTIONS

The commonest exception is the use of winter rules. These normally let you choose your lie – pick up your ball and place it on fairways and the aprons of greens. But they are not hard and fast rules because they are not part of the Rules of Golf. They are local rules made by the club committee.

Usually you can move the ball within 6in (15cm) – not nearer the hole – but the distance may vary in different golf clubs. You may also clean the ball when you lift it in these circumstances – after you have marked its position.

Sometimes clubs may continue their winter rules into spring and summer to take account of exceptional circumstances. These may include the condition of the fairways after a very dry summer.

Be careful to note when your club ends its winter rules. If you continue to choose your lie after the committee has ended the rule you lose a hole in matchplay or 2 strokes in strokeplay.

OBTAINING RELIEF

There are certain cases where you can help yourself quite legitimately under the rules. You can flatten the surface of the teeing ground of the hole you are playing in preparation for your stroke. You can lift and drop without penalty from casual water, holes made by burrowing animals and ground under repair.

You may also obtain relief without penalty from immovable obstructions, which include paths with

X **You can't move grass and brambles.**

✔ **If your ball lands in a difficult position you usually must play the ball as it lies or declare it unplayable, adding a 1 stroke** penalty and taking a drop. Don't flatten the surrounding ground or you are improving your lie and are liable for a 2 stroke penalty.

You are allowed to flatten the teeing ground of the hole you are about to play as part of your preparation to take a stroke.

manmade surfaces. You can drop the ball within one club length of the nearest point of relief which is not nearer the hole, except where that point puts you in a hazard or on a green. But make sure to check that there is not a local rule on the card which declares such paths 'integral parts of the course'.

If your shot from a bunker is impeded by damage caused by burrowing animals or casual water, you can take a drop but it must still be in the bunker.

There is no relief from damage by burrowing animals in a water hazard. Although this may sound odd, bear in mind that many hazards may be dry for parts of the year, leaving you the option of playing out of them.

Except in a hazard, you may remove loose impediments – stones, leaves, twigs – from around your ball, but you must be careful that the ball does not move as a result. If it does, you incur a penalty stroke and must replace the ball where it lay.

Bear in mind that you cannot remove loose impediments in bunkers. It sometimes seems quite natural to remove a leaf when you approach your ball in a bunker, but if you do so you suffer loss of hole in matchplay or 2 strokes in strokeplay. The only exception is that the rules allow you to remove enough matter to see a part of your ball.

On the green, but not elsewhere, sand and loose impediments may be removed.

Questions and answers

Folded divot

Q My ball came to rest in front of a divot which was folded over but still just attached to the ground. It clearly impeded my shot. Was I in order to remove it before playing my shot?

A No – this was not a loose impediment and removing or replacing it would have been improving your lie and line of your intended swing.

Embedded ball

Q In our last medal, I found my ball embedded in its own pitch mark on the fairway, and lifted it without penalty as the rules permit. Before dropping it, I repaired the pitch mark. My playing partner said I should not have done this, but surely I was correct?

A No – you were improving the area where your ball was to be dropped by adjusting its surface and you were subject to a 2 stroke penalty. If you had dropped the ball and it rolled back into your original pitch mark, you would have been allowed to re-drop it.

Out of bounds post

Q My partner in a foursomes matchplay competition removed a white post marking out of bounds because it was on his line of play. When our opponents pointed out that he was not allowed to do this, he replaced it carefully before playing his shot. Presumably there was no penalty?

A Yes, there was – you should have lost the hole. Your partner was in breach of the rule as soon as he moved the post and there was nothing he could do to avoid penalty.

Preparing line of play

Q My opponent was faced with a very tricky short pitch over a bunker, with the flag only 5yd (4.5m) beyond it. He went into the bunker and raked it level, just in case he was short with this delicate shot. Did this infringe the rules?

A Yes, his action was improving the line of play, which is forbidden.

Water relief

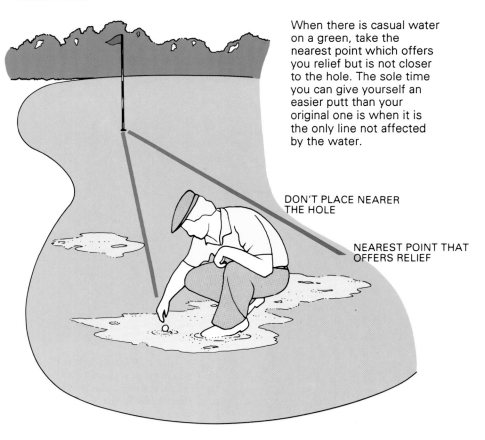

When there is casual water on a green, take the nearest point which offers you relief but is not closer to the hole. The sole time you can give yourself an easier putt than your original one is when it is the only line not affected by the water.

DON'T PLACE NEARER THE HOLE

NEAREST POINT THAT OFFERS RELIEF

Playing the wrong ball

All golfers play the wrong ball at some time in their careers. Although it's an easy mistake to make it's also a costly one – you are disqualified if you don't discover the error in time.

If you play a wrong ball you are liable to a 2 stroke penalty in strokeplay and the loss of a hole in matchplay. There is one important exception – there is no penalty for playing the wrong ball in a hazard.

You may not realize immediately that you have played a wrong ball.

It's quite common for a player to make several shots and notice the error only when putting out.

WHAT IT COSTS

In matchplay your first stroke with a wrong ball leads to the loss of a hole. In strokeplay the rules are quite merciful. The number of strokes played with a wrong ball on the same hole doesn't matter – the penalty remains 2 strokes.

Strokes played with the wrong ball don't count in your score. You correct your error by going back and playing the right ball. If you cannot find the original ball, you must play 3 off the tee and add the 2 penalty strokes to your score.

You must discover your mistake before playing from the next tee or leaving the putting green if on the last hole of your round. Otherwise you are disqualified.

If someone plays your ball, you place – not drop – a ball on the spot from which it was played by mistake. You don't take a penalty.

BE ALERT

Often one mistake leads to another when a wrong ball is played. For instance, if your opponent or fellow competitor in a twoball does not immediately recognize and declare the mistake, it is quite possible that you play the remaining ball without thinking.

It is your responsibility to play the correct ball at all times, so if you do this in strokeplay you are penalized 2 strokes. If you exchanged balls in matchplay, the first person to play a wrong ball loses the hole. If you can't determine this, the hole is played out with the balls exchanged.

A player who plays the wrong ball in fourball matchplay is eliminated from the hole, but his mistake does not affect his partner, who may go on without penalty.

If you find a ball embedded in a bunker, play it even if you're not sure that it's yours. There is no penalty for playing a wrong ball in a hazard so it won't cost you anything if you're mistaken.

Questions and answers: wrong ball

Missed stroke

Q In a difficult lie in the rough I aimed a stroke at what I thought was my ball, but missed it. In bending to remove a little loose grass, I realized that this was not in fact my ball. Was there any penalty?

A Yes – loss of a hole in matchplay and 2 strokes in strokeplay. You made a stroke at a wrong ball, even though you did not hit it.

Two balls

Q Playing a stroke from thick rough, my opponent hit an old ball which was hidden beneath his own ball, moving both of them a short distance. As he struck the hidden ball, did he play a wrong ball?

A No – he played a stroke with his own ball. The other ball was incidental to this, as for instance a hidden stone might have been.

Out of bounds

Q In a strokeplay competition on a course new to me, I put my tee shot on an adjoining fairway and played my second shot from there. We discovered that the card showed the fairway was in fact out of bounds on this hole. Had I played a wrong ball?

A Yes – a ball lying out of bounds is no longer in play and so is a wrong ball. You should have added 2 strokes to your score and gone back to play a second ball from the tee – in effect, your fifth shot.

Unplayable lie

Q I found a ball I thought was mine in a very difficult lie. I declared it unplayable and dropped it under penalty. Then I discovered that the ball was not in fact mine. Was I subject to a penalty?

A No, lifting and dropping a wrong ball costs nothing. Only if you played a shot at it would there be a penalty. You were entitled to go on looking for your own ball.

Exchanged balls

Q After we completed a hole I realized that my opponent and I had exchanged balls when we retrieved them from the hole. By this time my opponent had driven off from the next tee with my ball. Should he have lost the hole for playing a wrong ball?

A No – a ball played like that from the teeing ground is not a wrong ball, even if it does not belong to the player.

Bunker lie

Q I found what I thought was my ball lying very badly in the sandy face of a bunker. I declared it unplayable and dropped it in the bunker, under penalty of 1 stroke. I then played it out on to the green, but discovered when I went to clean it that it was not my ball. As I had ample opportunity to examine the ball when I lifted it, my companion thought that I was liable to a penalty, and I was inclined to agree with him. What is the correct decision?

A There is no penalty. The rules clearly exempt a player from penalty for playing a wrong ball in a hazard, even in the circumstances you describe.

pro tip

Place or drop?
Make sure you know the difference between *dropping* and *placing* a ball. You drop the ball by picking it up, holding it out at arm's length – either to the side or in front of you – and letting it go.

When you place the ball, you pick it up and place it on the ground in your chosen spot.

The rules state clearly when to drop and when to place and there are penalties for taking the wrong option. If your opponent plays your ball by mistake, you are allowed to place a new ball on the place where it was played. You do not take a drop.

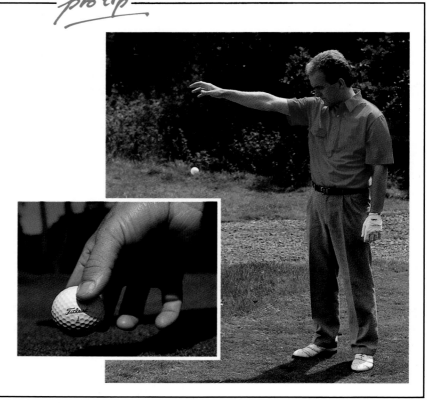

Dropping under penalty

**There are various times in golf when you need
to lift your ball under penalty.
Be aware of the options when you find yourself
in this situation.**

You take a drop under penalty when you hit a ball out of bounds, lose a ball, or when you decide that your ball is unplayable.

If you hit your ball out of bounds or lose it from the tee, you may tee the ball up for another attempt. You don't need to play from the exact spot of your previous shot – anywhere within the teeing area is fine. Elsewhere, you must drop a ball as near as possible to where the previous one was played. You add 1 penalty stroke.

UNPLAYABLE BALL

You may declare your ball unplayable at any point on the course except in or touching a water hazard. You don't have to accept anyone else's opinion – weigh up the chances of playing the ball successfully from a particular spot. Often you see high handicap players attempting shots which professionals would probably avoid by taking a drop.

Once you have decided that your

► **When you find yourself in an impossible lie it's often better to take a drop under penalty than to attempt to play the shot.**

One of your options is to take a drop two club lengths from the ball – but not nearer the hole. Use your longest club to gauge the lengths.

Once you have measured two club lengths, drop your ball – stand straight and hold your arm out either to your side or front.

ball is unplayable, you lift it under penalty of 1 shot. You then have three options:
● As with a lost or out of bounds ball, you can play your ball as near as possible to the spot where you played the last shot from. This option is useful if there is nowhere suitable to drop a ball – for instance if you're trapped deep in the woods.
● Drop your ball within two club lengths of where it lay, but not nearer the hole. If it rolls more than two club lengths from where it strikes the ground, you drop again. If it is again outside the limit, you place the ball as near as possible to the point where it hit the ground when re-dropped.

You can either take a drop two club lengths from your ball or you can walk back on the line of the ball until you find a free area to take a drop. Drop the ball on the line of your previous lie and the pin.

• Drop your ball behind the spot where it lay, keeping that point directly between the hole and the spot where you now drop it – you may go back as far as you like. This is a useful alternative to dropping within two club lengths, but sometimes it can take you deeper into trouble or beyond the bounds of the course.

If your ball lies in a bunker and you decide to declare it unplayable you can't use the options of two club lengths or going back on the ball's line. You must drop your ball in the bunker. When you lift your ball under penalty in this way, you may clean it if you want to. You can also play from where your last shot landed, under penalty.

If the ball touches you, your partner, your caddies or your equipment, whether before or after hitting the ground while you take a drop, it should be re-dropped.

Questions and answers: Drops with penalty

Drop selection

Q I declared my ball unplayable and dropped it within two club lengths as allowed under the rules. The ball rolled into an old divot mark and was again unplayable, though still within two club lengths and not nearer the hole. Could I have dropped the ball again without further penalty?

A Unfortunately not. Your ball was in play when you dropped it. You could have dropped it again, but only with a further stroke penalty. It pays to be as careful as you can in selecting the particular spot within the two club lengths where you decide to drop.

Easy way out

Q While on holiday in Scotland, I found my ball on a grassy island within a bunker. It had a horrid downhill lie, so I declared it unplayable. I took it back behind the bunker, exercising my right to take the ball back as far as I liked on a line between the hole and where my ball had been lying. My companion said that I should have dropped my ball in the bunker. Who was right?

A You were. Grass-covered ground within a bunker is not part of the bunker.

Tree lie

Q In Spain last year my ball lodged some way up in a palm tree. Though clearly visible and identifiable, it was obviously not playable, but more than two club lengths above the ground.

I went well back behind the tree to drop, keeping the spot where the ball had lodged on a line between me and the hole. Is there any way in which I could have dropped beneath the tree, where the ground was quite clear?

A Yes – you were entitled to drop a ball within two club lengths of the point on the ground immediately beneath the spot where the ball lay in the tree.

Escape from an island in a bunker by dropping on the ball's line.

Dropping without penalty

You can drop your ball without taking a penalty in certain circumstances. Make sure you know where you can take a free drop – it could make all the difference to your final score.

The most common times you can lift and drop your ball without taking a penalty are when it lands in casual water, ground under repair or holes made by burrowing animals. Many courses also have local rules requiring you to drop clear of young staked trees, without penalty.

It's not just the lie of the ball that you should consider. The rules allow you to take relief if your stance or the line of your intended swing are affected.

For instance, if you are standing in casual water to play your stroke, even though your ball itself is clear, you are entitled to relief if you want it. There doesn't have to be standing water – if it seeps up when you've taken your stance, it is said to be casual water and you can drop your ball without penalty.

ASK BEFORE LIFTING

How should you proceed when you have decided to take a free drop? You should ask your oppo-

◄ ▼ **Drainage ditches are always seen as ground cover under repair and if your ball lands there you are entitled to a free drop. If the area is not defined with white lines there will be a notice in the clubhouse with details of the ground under repair.**

nent in matchplay or your marker in strokeplay to confirm your right to a drop without penalty before you lift the ball. If you lift without their permission you may end up with a penalty if they dispute your right to a free drop.

You drop the ball in the same way as you would in any circumstance – standing straight, holding the ball at shoulder height and arm's length, and dropping it.

When you are taking relief without penalty, you select the nearest spot on the course which gives you relief from the situation. Drop your ball within a club length – but not nearer the hole.

Bear in mind that it may not always be a good idea to take relief, even when it is available without penalty.

For instance, if you discover your ball in ground under repair you may feel that you have a better lie than you would if you lifted and dropped your ball. In this case, you are normally free to play the ball as it lies. But sometimes a local rule makes you take relief to preserve the course.

RE-DROPPING THE BALL

When you drop the ball it may roll up to a distance of two club lengths from where it hits the ground provided it doesn't finish nearer the hole. You can re-drop if the ball is:

- nearer the hole, or has rolled into a hazard – or out of a hazard when you were taking relief within one. When you drop from a hazard, your ball must stay in it.
- on a putting green.
- out of bounds.
- back in the situation from which you are taking relief.

If it rolls into one of these situations for a second time you then place the ball on the spot where it struck the ground when re-dropped.

Questions and answers: free drops

Sly spin

Q My opponent stood erect, held the ball at shoulder height and arm's length, and prepared to drop his ball without penalty. However, in dropping it he deliberately put spin on the ball with his fingers, to try to propel the ball into the best possible lie. Is this allowed by the rules?

A No – if he lifted the ball and re-dropped it correctly there would not be a penalty. But as he dropped it incorrectly he should have taken a 1 stroke penalty.

Which club?

Q My opponent found his ball in the edge of woodland. He used his driver to measure two club lengths, but when he dropped his ball it ran into a difficult lie. Using his putter to measure, he then demonstrated that the ball had rolled outside the two club length limit, and claimed that he could therefore re-drop it. I thought that as it was still within two driver lengths he should play it from where it lay after the first drop. Was I correct?

A Yes. A player may use any club in his bag to measure his club lengths, but he must continue to use the same one he has chosen in any particular situation.

Unauthorized lift

Q My opponent marked and lifted my ball on the green without any request from me to do so. Is there a penalty for doing this?

A Yes – he may lift your ball only with your authority. He should have been penalized a stroke for lifting a ball when he was not allowed to do so.

Dropping zone

Q Behind our 18th green there is a wire netting fence which is the boundary of the course. Several times during the summer balls have come to rest against this netting. There is nowhere to drop within two club lengths, and even if it were possible to go back keeping the spot where the ball had rested in line with the hole, this would be out of bounds. Should the club create a permanent dropping zone to cope with the situation?

A Although a local rule to create a dropping zone is possible, the R and A approve of such solutions only in exceptional circumstances. The dropping zones you see on television in use at professional tournaments are temporary measures forced on the organizers because grandstands take up space. There is the option of playing again from where the previous shot was played, and adding a 1 stroke penalty.

▲ Some clubs have dropping zones behind a large area of ground under repair. You can take a free drop within two club lengths of the sign if your ball lands there.

Ball unfit for play

**If you want to change your ball during a round
be aware of the rules that apply
– you can pick up penalties if you lift your ball
without informing your fellow player.**

You don't need a reason to change your ball **between holes**. Tell your fellow player and make sure your new ball is a type approved by the R and A. It doesn't have to be the same make. Although the PGA European Tour currently insists that a substituted ball should be one of exactly the same make and type, that is a rule of the tour and not a rule of golf.

If you want to change your ball **while playing a hole** it must be unfit for play and you must ask your fellow player to confirm this before you change it.

A ball is unfit for play if it is visibly cut, cracked or out of shape. It is not unfit for play if it's just scratched or scraped or because its paint is damaged or discoloured. Nor is a ball unfit if it's covered in mud or dirt.

Occasionally a solid ball breaks into pieces when you play a stroke. If that happens, replay the stroke with another ball, dropping the new one where the original ball lay. There is no penalty.

WHAT YOU DO

While playing a hole you may lift your ball without penalty to check whether it is unfit, but you must first tell your fellow player what

▼ **You can lift your ball and examine it for damage at any time during your round. Make sure you tell your fellow player what you're doing or you could pick up a 1 stroke penalty. You can change your ball between holes whether or not it's damaged, but if you want to change a ball during a hole you and your partners must agree it's unfit for play.**

you're about to do. If you lift your ball without announcing your intention, or you don't give your fellow player a chance to examine the ball, you incur a 1 stroke penalty.

If there's agreement that your ball is unfit for play you can substitute another ball. You place – not drop – the new ball on the spot where the original one lay. If the other player wants to dispute your claim that your ball is unfit, it must be done before you play another ball. If your ball is found to be fit for play, you replace it and carry on playing without penalty.

DON'T CLEAN IT

When you lift the ball you may not clean it to find out if it's unfit for play – if you do you are penalized a stroke. This means that if you think a crack or a cut is covered by mud, you cannot remove the mud to check. If you cannot establish that the ball is damaged without cleaning it, you must replace the original ball and play on with it until the hole is completed.

Fit or unfit?

Your ball is unfit for play if you can see that it's misshapen or there are cracks or cuts on it. A damaged ball can be changed during a hole as long as your fellow player agrees it is unfit.

If your ball is scuffed, scratched or muddy it is not officially unfit for play and you must continue to play the hole. You can clean, examine and change your ball between holes.

Questions and answers: unfit ball

Illegal ball

Q When my ball was clearly damaged during the play of a hole, I substituted another I had found earlier in the round. I played only one stroke before realizing that the ball was smaller than standard and replaced the illegal ball with a correct one. I ended the round with a very good medal score, but I was disqualified. This seemed a very harsh penalty for one incorrect stroke. Was it correct?

A Yes – unfortunately the rules of golf are often harsh but this was the correct decision. Always check the size of the ball you play. The rules have been changed to standardize the size of balls so watch out for any old small balls which may still be lurking in the bottom of your bag or hiding in the rough on a course.

Internal damage?

Q My opponent hit a tee shot which swung sharply in flight. With my consent he lifted and examined his ball. We could find no external damage and the ball was not out of shape. He said that the behaviour of the ball indicated that it must be damaged internally, but I thought he had merely hit a bad hook. Should he have been allowed to substitute another ball?

A No, a substitution was not in order. Whether he had hooked the ball or there was any internal damage is irrelevant. The rules say that the ball must be *visibly* damaged before it can be replaced during the course of play. Your opponent should have completed the play of the hole with his original ball. He could then change it between holes if he wished.

Re-using a ball

Q My opponent damaged his ball, declared it unfit for play and substituted another one. He then put two balls out of bounds and lost them. Because he was running short of good balls, he played the damaged ball again at the next hole. Was he allowed to do this?

A Yes – but he may not declare it unfit for play again, unless it suffers further damage.

Plugged ball

Q My opponent's ball was plugged in a hazard. He insisted on lifting it to check whether it had been damaged, after telling me that this was what he was doing. Was he allowed to lift his ball in this situation?

A Yes, you can lift a ball anywhere on the course, even in a hazard. The substitute ball – or the original one if it's undamaged – must be replaced in exactly the same lie.

Bunkers

**What do you do if your ball is deeply embedded in
a bunker, or if a stone is in the
way of your ball? As usual, the rules are quite
specific and it pays to know them.**

The state and depth of the sand in a bunker may be quite important in deciding the type of shot you choose to play. But beware – you must not test the condition of the sand in a hazard before you take your shot.

FEET PLACING

You often see players wriggling their feet before they play, sometimes so much that the sand almost reaches the tops of their shoes.

The rules allow you to place your feet firmly when you take your stance but forbid you to build a stance by deliberately packing sand under your feet. If a player gains some idea of how firm and how deep the sand is in the bunker as he takes his stance, that is his good fortune.

You are not allowed to touch loose impediments in a bunker, but you often see players removing stones from hazards without being penalized.

This is because some clubs have local rules allowing you to remove stones from bunkers on their courses. When courses have these local rules they are normally printed on the back of the card of the course.

Most clubs in Britain have a local rule regarding stones in bunkers, but be careful – there are exceptions. A leading amateur lost a hole in an important match in the 1990 English Amateur Championship because he assumed he was allowed to remove a stone in the bunker. The club in question had no such local rule.

Bunkers and water hazards provide the only opportunity for you to play a wrong ball without being penalized. It may sometimes be difficult to identify your ball in a bunker, particularly when more than one ball lands there.

You must not lift the ball to identify it in these circumstances, as you may do elsewhere on the course. Instead, play out the one you think is yours. If you then find the ball is not yours, there is no penalty. If it belongs to an opponent

▼ **Gordon Brand jnr was penalized 2 strokes for smoothing out his footprints before playing his second bunker shot in the 1991 Volvo Open. Rules officials later admitted making a mistake and restored the pro to his rightful position.**

or fellow competitor, you should replace the ball as near as possible to the original lie.

BURIED BALL

Sometimes your ball is completely buried in a bunker. The rules allow you to search for it, even using a club to do so. Try to expose only part of the ball. But if you accidentally expose more or dislodge the ball, there is no penalty – replace the ball and cover it with sand until just a small part is exposed to allow you to see where it is.

When a bunker has casual water in it and your ball lands there, you can lift and drop your ball without penalty. Choose the nearest spot in the bunker which gives you maximum relief and is not nearer the hole.

Sometimes you may find that the whole of a bunker is filled with water. You then have two options – you can proceed as above, dropping your ball at the point in the bunker not nearer the hole where you think the water is shallowest.

Alternatively you can drop the ball outside the bunker, keeping the point where it lay directly between you and the hole, under penalty of 1 shot.

▲ If you find casual water in a bunker you can take a free drop within the hazard. Make sure you choose a spot not nearer the hole before you drop your ball.

▶ Many courses – especially in Britain – have local rules allowing players to remove stones in a bunker. But don't throw out a stone without checking the card of the course carefully, otherwise you could be penalized.

Questions and answers: bunker play

Rake row

Q My opponent took a rake with him into a bunker so that he could smooth his footprints after he had played his shot. Before he played, he deliberately struck the handle of the rake into the sand. Was this allowed?

A No – he was testing the condition of the sand. He should have lost the hole in matchplay or been penalized 2 strokes in strokeplay. The same penalty would apply if a player pushed his umbrella into the sand.

Club choice

Q I took my stance in a fairway bunker, then decided that the club I had in my hand was too straight faced to clear the lip. I left the bunker to change the club and then took my stance again in the same place. My opponent

said I was breaking the rules by testing the condition of the hazard at my first visit. Was he correct?

A No – there's nothing in the rules to stop you deciding to change your club or taking your stance twice in a bunker.

Pretend play

Q While waiting to play a bunker shot, my opponent went to another part of the hazard, took a firm stance, and simulated his bunker shot, without using his club. Was this allowed?

A No – he was breaking the rules as he was testing the sand.

Equipment in bunker

Q My opponent placed his bag of clubs in a bunker before playing his shot. Surely this was against the rules?

A No, it was quite permissible. The exceptions listed under the rules allow a player to place his or her clubs in a bunker, provided he or she does nothing to test the state of the sand or improve the lie of the ball.

Conscientious caddy

Q When I was playing in a final last year my caddie, without permission, raked the sand in a bunker before I played my second shot from the trap. Presumably as this was matchplay I should have lost the hole?

A Provided that nothing is done which improves your lie or assists you in your play of the hole afterwards, you – or your caddie – can rake a bunker before playing a second shot.

On the green

**The putting green has special rules that dictate everything
from the line of your putt to
moving loose impediments and repairing pitch marks.**

The green is the area of the golf hole especially prepared for putting. It does not include the fringe. Your ball is on the green when any part of it touches the putting surface. This can be important as different rules apply depending on whether you are just on or just off the green.

For instance, you may mark your ball, lift it and clean it once you are on the green. Elsewhere you will normally have to play the ball as it lies, unless preferred lie or winter rules are in force.

You must place a ball marker – a small coin or similar object – immediately behind the ball before you lift it. If your fellow player thinks the marker interferes with his play or stance, you can move it to one side or the other – usually one or more putter heads away to clear the path.

If your ball or ball marker is accidentally moved in the course of lifting or marking, there is no penalty, and the ball or marker should be replaced.

LINE OF PUTT

You may repair old pitch marks or old refilled holes, but nothing else. This means that you may not repair spike marks.

Removal of sand, soil or loose impediments is allowed. Do this by picking them up or by brushing them aside with your hand or club, but don't press them down.

When you measure to see which ball is nearer to the hole, or when you lift your ball, you may touch the line of the putt. Grounding the

▼ **Sam Torrance was caught out by a green rule in the 1990 English Open. His ball teetered on the edge of the 10th hole and eventually fell in – but he was deemed to have waited too long, and had to add a penalty stroke. It was an important ruling, for he eventually lost the event to Mark James in a play-off.**

Questions and answers

Checking the turf

Q Not being sure whether a tuft of grass was attached to the ground or not, I brushed it lightly with my hand, and found it was attached. My opponent maintained that I was in breach of the rules for trying to remove something which was not a loose impediment. Was she right?

A No – provided you restored the raised tuft to its original position before you putted, you were entitled to find out whether such a natural object on the line of your putt was loose or not.

Using equipment

Q My opponent removed loose impediments from the line of his putt by brushing them aside with his cap at one hole and with a towel at the next. Was this allowed?

A No – the rules let a player brush aside loose impediments on the line of a putt only with his hand or a club.

Touching the green

Q My opponent was preparing to putt from the apron of the green when his caddie touched the putting surface to indicate the line of his putt. Was this allowed?

A Yes – the rule about touching the green to indicate the line of play applies only when the player's ball lies on the green.

Dewy green

Q Am I allowed to brush dew from the line of my putt?

A No – dew is not a loose impediment.

Accidental breach

Q I know that a player should not step on the line of his opponent's putt. But is there a penalty if you do so by accident?

A There is no penalty for accidentally stepping on your opponent's line.

Deeply embedded

Q I found an embedded acorn on the line of my putt. I removed it, lifted it, and repaired the indentation it had left. Was this in order?

A No – you were allowed to remove the acorn as a loose impediment, since it was so solidly embedded, but you should not have repaired the indentation it had left.

Showing the way

Q When asked to attend the flag for my putt, my caddie took out the pin and rested it upright immediately behind the hole. This was because he was afraid of it sticking in the hole. My opponent claimed the hole because she maintained the green should not have been touched. Was she right?

A Yes – your caddie could have been illegally indicating the line of your putt. He is allowed to show the line only by pointing the flag at a spot.

Watch your spikes
Don't feel tempted to tap down spike marks on a green – even if you have made them yourself. A mistake of this kind will cost you 2 strokes in strokeplay or the loss of the hole in a matchplay competition.

◄ ▼ **You can remove loose impediments such as sand or bits of grass from the line of your putt. But make sure to use your hand or your club to brush them away – not your towel or other equipment.**

club lightly in front of the ball is also allowed when you address your putt, but you must not press anything down.

Apart from these exceptions you must not touch the line of a putt.

Either you or your partner or one of your caddies may point out what you think is the line of a putt. But you must not touch the green in the process, or place anything on the green which would help with the line of a putt.

On the other hand, if there is a leaf or similar object on the green which you think will help you with the line of a putt, there is no obligation to lift it.

Do not test the surface or speed of a green by rolling a ball or roughening the surface. If you casually knock away a putt which you have conceded, there is no penalty, provided that you were merely returning the ball to the player rather than making a deliberate attempt to test the speed of the green.

HITTING THE PUTT

Standing astride your ball to putt is forbidden. Don't stand with either foot touching the line of the putt or an extension of that line behind the ball.

What happens if your ball overhangs the lip of the hole and looks as though it might drop in at any second? You are allowed to walk up to the hole without reasonable delay, then you are allowed to wait ten seconds.

If by then the ball has not dropped, it is deemed at rest and you must tap it in. If the ball falls in after the time limit and you don't remove it and tap it in, you're penalized a stroke.

Out of bounds and lost ball

**Understand the rules and you're less likely to fall foul
of them. The loathed stroke and distance, for
example, may seem harsh, but it helps protect fair play.**

When you hit your ball **out of bounds** the procedure is straightforward. You go back and play another ball from as near as possible to the same spot, counting the stroke which put you out of bounds and adding a penalty stroke – what is traditionally called stroke and distance. For instance, if your first shot put the ball out of bounds you are playing three with the second ball.

A ball is out of bounds only when all of it lies within the prohibited area. Where the area is defined by a line on the ground, that line is also out of bounds. You may stand out of bounds to play a shot when the ball is lying within bounds.

If you are playing another ball from the tee you may place it anywhere within the teeing area. You are allowed to tee the ball up as you normally do. Elsewhere on the course you drop the ball as near as possible to the spot where the previous one was played, making sure as usual that you are not nearer the hole.

The rules – and the penalty – for a **lost ball** are much the same as for out of bounds. But you need to remember exactly when a ball is officially lost.

Your ball is considered lost once you have looked for it for more than five minutes, even if you then find it. It is also lost if you decide to put another ball into play, even when you don't search for it. Even if you or someone else finds the ball immediately, once you have chosen to put another ball in play the original is still lost as far as the rules are concerned.

You need to be very careful before playing a second ball. If you intend it to be a provisional, tell your opponent or fellow competitor. If you simply put a second ball down and play it, this becomes the ball in play even if you find your original one.

A ball is also considered lost when you play a stroke with a provisional ball from nearer to the hole than where the original one lies. In these circumstances, even if you or someone else finds the original ball, you cannot then play it but must continue with your provisional since this has become the ball in play.

TROUBLE SPOTS

On some courses in winter it is quite possible to have large areas of casual water where you might easily lose a ball. When your ball is lost in **casual water** or **ground under repair** you are allowed to take relief without penalty.

You can give yourself a free drop within a club length of what

◄ You can stand out of bounds – usually defined by a fence, posts or lines on the ground – to play your ball when it is lying within bounds. But you can't play a ball that's come to rest out of bounds – you have to drop the ball under a 1 stroke penalty from where you last played your shot.

you think is the nearest point of relief. The only condition is that there must be what the regulations call reasonable evidence that the ball really is lost there rather than somewhere else on the course.

If your ball goes into a **water hazard** you don't need to find it – in fact, this may be impossible – but again there must be reasonable evidence that it was lost there. You drop another ball and take a stroke penalty.

▶ **The Atlantic Ocean catches many tee shots on the hazardous 9th at Turnberry. Because the sea is not out of bounds, in the unlikely event of you finding your ball you can play it off the rocks. Always thoroughly check your score card before you start a round to find out what areas are defined as out of bounds or hazards.**

Questions and answers: lost balls

Second ball

Q I searched for my second shot in deep rough for a moment, then went back and dropped another ball. My opponent then found my ball, before I played and within the five minute period. I abandoned the dropped ball and played my original one. Was I correct?

A No – your second ball was in play as soon as you dropped it, and the original one was lost. A ball dropped through the green is in play as soon as it is dropped.

Which ball?

Q My opponent searched briefly for his tee shot, then went back and teed another ball. Before he played it, and within the five minute period, I found his ball. I thought he could still abandon the teed ball and play the original, but he thought his teed ball was in play and he had to play it. Who was correct?

A You were. The teed ball was not in play until he had made a stroke at it.

Declare your intention

Q My opponent hit his tee shot and it vanished into what looked like out of bounds. Cursing, he teed up another but sliced it into rough. We then discovered his original still on the fairway and he continued the hole with this ball. Was he allowed to?

A No. As he didn't properly declare his intention of playing a provisional, the second ball became the one in play. Your opponent would now have played three shots – the original tee shot, the second ball and a penalty shot.

Helpful spectator

Q In a recent match I shanked my tee shot into trees in front of the tee. I announced a provisional ball and hit this well down the middle of the fairway.

After looking for the original ball for one minute, I abandoned the search and went to play the provisional. Before I reached that ball, a spectator found the original within the five minute time limit. What was the ruling?

A Your original ball was the one in play. The lost ball was found within five minutes, and you had not played a stroke at the provisional after abandoning the search for the original.

Reasonable evidence

Q In a recent match I lost my ball and assumed that it must have landed in a water hazard as it couldn't be seen anywhere on the fairway. My opponent objected, as neither of us had seen the ball splashing into the water. Advice please.

A If there was no rough or other area where the ball may have been lost, and the ball was nowhere to be seen on the fairway, it's reasonable to assume it was in the water hazard. Seeing a ball splash into the hazard isn't always counted as reasonable evidence – it could skip out. But if the ball can't be anywhere else *but* in the hazard, you have reasonable evidence.

Unplayable ball

**Sooner or later in golf you are bound to find
your ball in an unplayable lie.
You must be quite clear on how to deal with this
situation as the penalties are severe.**

If you think your ball is impossible to play - for instance if you find it halfway up a tree or in dense thorny rough - you can declare it unplayable and drop the ball under penalty of 1 stroke.

Bear in mind that you are the sole judge of when your ball is unplayable. This is important as what might be quite playable to a competent golfer may prove to be too difficult for a beginner.

As a general rule it's wiser to err on the side of caution. High handicappers often attempt shots which professionals would not try. Often it's better to take a stroke penalty and give yourself a reasonable lie.

You can declare your ball unplayable anywhere on the golf course, except where it touches a hazard. It costs you 1 stroke to do so and then you must choose any one of the three options available to you.

HOW TO PROCEED

You can go back to where you played your last shot and take another shot, or drop your ball within two club lengths of where it lies. If you prefer, you can drop your ball as far as you like behind the unplayable ball's original poor lie.

If you choose the third option you must keep the point where you drop the ball between you

Deep heathery rough is very tricky to escape from, so assess the lie carefully before you attempt to play it. Sometimes lies like this are best left to the professionals. High handicappers would be better off declaring their ball unplayable and taking a 1 stroke penalty.

Questions and answers

No recovery

Q When we played in Spain recently, my companion hit his tee shot into a deep canyon, which was not a water hazard. He immediately declared it unplayable and played another ball from the tee as his third stroke. Was he able to declare unplayable a ball which had not been found?

A Yes he was. He was exercising the first of the three options he is allowed.

How many shots?

Q My fellow competitor in our last monthly medal hit his tee shot deep into the woods. He played a provisional ball, which went into the same woods. He then declared his first ball unplayable, said he was abandoning his provisional ball, and hit a third shot from the tee to the middle of the fairway.

He did not search for either of the first two balls - maintaining that his third ball was the ball in play and he was lying three. He argued that as he had declared his first ball unplayable before playing the third one, the second was only a provisional and now irrelevant. The committee subsequently ruled that he should have been playing five with the third ball. Who was correct?

A The committee was. Unless the original ball was found, the provisional ball became the one in play. So when that ball was abandoned your friend was playing his fifth shot.

Miss-hit

Q My partner's tee shot came to rest in the roots of a tree. She attempted to play the ball there, but hit only an air shot. She then declared the ball unplayable. Could she have returned to the tee and played four from there, as the ball had not been disturbed?

A No - an air shot counts as a stroke. The first option under the unplayable ball rule allows the player to play from the spot where the previous shot was played. The previous shot in this case was played from the roots of the tree, not the tee. Having declared the ball unplayable, she had to drop either within two club lengths or behind the tree roots, keeping that spot in line with the hole.

Bunker drop

Q My friend, a low handicap player, declared his ball unplayable on a steep downhill bank near the green. He dropped his ball within two club lengths, but in a bunker since he thought he had a better chance of getting near the flag with a bunker shot then a pitch from behind the bunker. Was he allowed to drop in the bunker deliberately?

A Yes - he was allowed to drop his ball in a hazard.

Rock deflection

Q When we were playing in Spain, my ball hit a rock and bounced further from the hole than the spot from which I had just played. I declared it unplayable. Was I allowed to play from the spot I had just played, even though it was nearer the hole than where the ball now lay?

A In these circumstances you can play from the spot where the ball originally lay, even if it's nearer the hole.

Mistaken breach

Q In a recent medal, my companion having declared her ball unplayable in a bunker, mistakenly dropped it outside the bunker. We did not realize at the time that she was in breach of the rules, so the error was not corrected. What was the penalty?

A Disqualification. She would have been allowed to drop the ball outside the bunker if she had gone back to the spot from which her previous shot was played.

and the hole. This is often a useful choice when you are in a copse of trees with open ground behind.

If you declare your ball unplayable in a bunker, you must drop it in the hazard unless you choose to play again from the place where you took the previous shot.

When you lift and drop an unplayable ball, you may clean it before dropping it.

Breaking the unplayable ball rules will lose you the hole in matchplay. In strokeplay, you take a 2 stroke penalty.

▶ **Sometimes your ball finds such an impossible lie that you have no option but to declare it unplayable. If your ball lands in a tree, for instance, accept your penalty and drop your ball free of interference.**

RULES TO HELP YOU

A golfer who knows the rules possesses a real advantage. Here, we take a look at a few everyday situations where specific rules allow you to move your ball away from obstacles that shouldn't be there. Saving strokes in this way can make the difference between winning and losing.

**An erratic driver at times,
Crenshaw owes part of his success
to his brilliant recovery play.
He always assesses the shot
coolly and calmly before playing
the stroke.**

Obstructions

What do you do when your ball lands under a parked car or on a bench? The ruling on movable and immovable obstructions is quite logical – find out how to gain relief.

You are normally entitled to relief without penalty from obstructions – defined as anything artificial, including the artificial surfaces and sides of roads and paths.

There are three exceptions, and for these you cannot claim relief. The first two concern **out of bounds obstructions**. There is no relief from any objects defining out of bounds, such as walls, fences, stakes and railings. And you can't claim relief from any immovable object – such as a building – which is out of bounds.

These may not seem important exceptions, but remember that you are allowed to stand out of bounds to play a ball which is just in bounds. You quite often find that an out of bounds fence, or a post outside it, prevents a swing at a ball that would otherwise be playable. In this situation it's usually best to declare the ball unplayable and drop it with a penalty of a shot.

The third exception is the one that often causes confusion. This is the clause which allows the committee to declare what would normally be an obstruction an **integral part of the course**. The most famous example of this exception is the tarmac road which runs behind the 17th green of the Old Course at St Andrews in Scotland.

Many golfers who are used to enjoying relief from roads on their own courses cannot understand why they see professionals having to play from the road at the headquarters of golf. The reason is that the committee of the club have declared this particular road to be an integral part of the course.

This rule underlines the important point that when playing at an unfamiliar course you should first check the card of the course carefully for local rules. You must know if the committee of the club has taken advantage of its powers to declare what would normally be obstructions as integral parts of the course where no relief is available.

▼ **You are usually allowed relief if your ball lands on a road, but on some courses – such as the 17th at St Andrews Old – the road is declared an integral part of the course. Always check your score card before claiming relief from obstructions – if your ball lands on an integral part of the course you cannot claim relief.**

MOVABLE OBSTRUCTIONS

When an obstruction is movable – a bench, for instance – you take relief from it in one of two ways. If your ball does not lie in or on the obstruction, you may remove the object. If your ball moves, there is no penalty – you simply replace it.

If your ball lies in or on the obstruction you may lift your ball without penalty, and move the object. On the green you then place your ball; anywhere else on the course you drop it. You do this so that the ball finishes as near as possible to the spot directly under where the ball lay, but not nearer the hole. You may clean your ball when you lift it.

► **If your ball lands near a post defining out of bounds you cannot claim relief. You must not move the post to play your shot, even if it hampers your swing. If you do move it, you lose the hole in matchplay and 2 strokes in strokeplay.**

Questions and answers

Movable decision

Q I cannot find an exact definition in the rules of golf of a movable obstruction. Can you help?

A You're quite right. The rules of golf do not give a definition of a movable obstruction, presumably because the term is thought to be self explanatory. But a decision of the R and A says that an obstruction is movable if it may be moved without undue effort, without delaying play and without damaging the property of the course.

Steep steps

Q Are wooden steps on a steep bank an obstruction?

A Yes, they are – you can take relief from these sorts of wooden steps. But if steps are simply cut into the bank and not artificially covered they are not obstructions. If your ball lies on earthen steps you must play the ball as it lies or take relief under penalty.

Parked car

Q What happens if a ball comes to rest under a parked car?

A If the car is easily movable, it should be treated as a movable obstruction – so the car should be moved and the ball played as it lies. If the car cannot readily be moved it should be treated as an immovable obstruction. Severiano Ballesteros got relief from just such a situation during his famous first Open Championship victory at Lytham in 1979.

Natural surface

Q Is a path which has been surfaced with wood chips an obstruction?

A Yes – wood chips, ash, gravel and the like are artificial surfaces just as much as concrete or tar in this context so you can take relief from them. As always you need to check the card to make sure that the committee has not exercised its right to declare such a path an integral part of the course – in which case, you cannot take relief without penalty.

Wooden planks

Q Is wood which has been made into planks an obstruction?

A Yes, planks are deemed an obstruction – unless they are a part of the course – and you can claim relief if your ball lands on or beside them.

Abandoned ball

Q In a match earlier this year my ball came to rest against an abandoned ball in the rough. I could not treat this as a loose impediment because my ball would have moved. How should I have proceeded?

A An abandoned ball is a movable obstruction. You could have moved it and dropped your ball as near as possible to where it originally lay. You could also have replaced your ball without penalty if it moved.

Obstructions 2

**You are entitled to relief when an immovable obstruction
interferes with your shot,
but don't pick up your ball and take relief without
checking the rules thoroughly.**

You can claim relief from an **immovable obstruction** – something fixed and artificial such as a bridge or marker post – when your ball lies in or on the object, or so close to it that it gets in the way of your stance or the area of your swing.

There is no relief from objects which define out of bounds, or from any part of an immovable obstruction that is out of bounds. The committee can also declare any construction to be an integral part of the course – this means that there is no relief from it.

You must check the card of the course carefully to make sure that roads and buildings which would normally entitle you to relief have not been declared integral parts of the course. If they have, the information is on the card.

The fact that the obstruction is on your line of sight does not entitle you to relief. You may have seen professional golfers receiving line of sight relief from objects such as advertising hoardings, but that is an official's decision, because hoardings are temporary and abnormal additions to the course.

TAKING RELIEF

Before you claim relief from an immovable obstruction **through the green** you must find a point on the course nearest to where the ball lies without crossing over, through or under the obstruction.

Say your ball lands beside a fixed bench. You cannot measure a club length *under* the bench – you must take relief clear of the object. The point must be clear of interference, not nearer the hole, and not in a hazard or on a green. When you have found a satisfactory spot you lift the ball and drop it within a club length of this point.

▼ **If your ball lands on a sprinkler head you are entitled to a free drop as the sprinkler is an immovable obstruction. Lift the ball and drop it within one club length from the obstruction but not nearer the hole or on the green.**

The rule about not crossing over, through or under the obstruction does not apply to artificial surfaces of roads, or when the ball lies in or on the object. If your ball lies on a road you can bring it back across the road to find the *nearest* point of relief not nearer the hole.

To claim relief from an immovable obstruction in a **bunker** – perhaps your ball lies beside the exposed concrete wall of a man-made bunker – the ball must be dropped in the bunker.

If your ball lies in or touches a **water hazard** there is no relief without penalty from interference by an immovable obstruction.

▶ **To claim relief it has to be your stance or swing that is affected by the immovable obstruction, not your line of sight. In this case the position of the barn allows the player to swing freely so he can't take relief, despite the fact that he is unable to see his target.**

PIN OUT OF VIEW

BLOCKED LINE

PLAY TO LEFT

Questions and answers: immovable objects

Double trouble

Q My opponent's ball was just in bounds but his shot was affected by the boundary fence, from which the rules gave him no relief. But a wall of a building near the fence interfered with his swing. He claimed that he was allowed to take relief from the immovable obstruction, even though this would also give him relief from the fence. Was he correct?

A Yes, he could claim relief. It was his good fortune that relief from the immovable obstruction also gave him a clear shot from the boundary fence.

Fairway drop

Q My opponent found his ball in the rough, with his stance impeded by an immovable obstruction. He took relief and dropped the ball in accordance with the rules, but on the fairway. Was this allowed?

A Yes – there is no distinction in the rules between fairway

and rough. Both are covered by the term 'through the green'.

Swing interference

Q My ball came to rest just in bounds. I could play it by standing out of bounds, except that an immovable artificial object – a stone post – situated out of bounds interfered with my swing. Could I have claimed relief?

A No – any immovable object which is off the course is not an obstruction, and there is no relief from it.

Clubhouse chip

Q I heard of a golfer who hit his ball into the clubhouse, which had not been declared out of bounds or an integral part of the course. He then opened a window and chipped his ball on to the nearby putting green. Surely this was not in order?

A Yes, it was! The clubhouse was an immovable obstruction. But any part of it designed to be movable – such as

a window or door – may be moved provided it can be done without undue delay. Even if the clubhouse has been declared an integral part of the course, the same principle applies. Similarly, a player finding his ball near a barn or shed may open the doors to play a shot through the building.

Line of sight

Q My ball came to rest behind the corner of a tractor shed which was an immovable obstruction. As this interfered with my swing, I was clearly allowed relief from it. But the shed was also on the line of sight, from which the rules allow no relief. When I dropped the ball to give myself a clear stance I also gained a clear line of sight for my shot. Was this permissible?

A Yes, you were clearly allowed relief from the immovable obstruction. The fact that this also gave you line of sight relief was simply good luck.

Casual water

**Most golfers are aware that they can claim relief
without penalty from casual water.
But there is often uncertainty about what exactly
it is and how relief should be taken.**

Casual water is any *temporary accumulation* of water on the course which is visible before or after you take your stance to hit a shot. It may occur anywhere on the course, except in what is already defined as a water hazard. Dew is not casual water, but you have the choice of treating snow and ice as either casual water or loose impediments.

Your ball does not have to lie in the water for you to claim relief. If the water affects your stance you may take relief even if the ball is lying clear of the pool. Once you are on the green, you are allowed relief if the water is on the line of your putt.

But what about borderline cases? What is classed as casual water? Soft, mushy turf is not casual water, unless water is visible on the surface before or after you take your stance.

That is the key point – water must be visible on the surface of the ground. Often you find that water wells up around the soles of your shoes when you take your stance, even when it wasn't previously visible. If so, you are entitled to relief. But you must take your normal stance – pressing down hard with one foot to make water appear is cheating.

On many courses water overflows from water hazards, particularly during the winter months. Players are sometimes uncertain whether this is casual water or part of the hazard. There should be no difficulty, because the limits of the

▼ **The greenkeepers sweep the greens up after a downpour during the US Masters. Though heavy rain can wreak havoc, don't be tempted to clear casual water away from your line when you're on a green – you lose a hole in matchplay or 2 strokes in strokeplay. Instead, choose the nearest point of relief not nearer the hole.**

Questions and answers

Out of bounds

Q My ball was just in bounds but I had to stand outside the course to play it. I found that when I took my stance I was in casual water. Was I entitled to relief?

A Relief couldn't be claimed – the definition of casual water states that it must occur on the course.

Water on the line

Q On a very wet green there was no casual water visible on the line of my putt. But when I walked forward beside the line I could see water welling up around my feet. Could I take relief?

A No – casual water must be already visible on your line or round your feet when you take your stance for you to claim relief.

Clearing the way

Q In a recent match my opponent found his ball just short of the green. He then mopped up a pool of casual water on the green before taking his shot. Was this allowed?

A This was against the rules. Your opponent should have lost the hole for improving his line of play. Even if his ball was on the green he mustn't mop up the water – though he could move his ball to get relief from water on his line.

Improving your line

Q Am I allowed to brush small amounts of casual water off the line of my putt when my ball lies on the green?

A Casual water is not a loose impediment so mustn't be removed in this way. You would lose the hole in matchplay or suffer a 2 stroke penalty in strokeplay for touching the line of your putt.

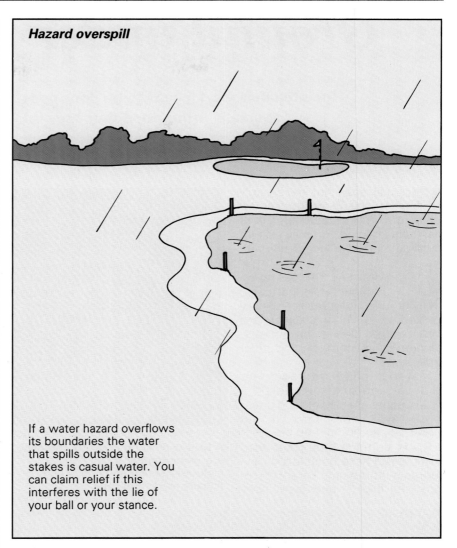

Hazard overspill

If a water hazard overflows its boundaries the water that spills outside the stakes is casual water. You can claim relief if this interferes with the lie of your ball or your stance.

water hazard are properly defined by yellow or red posts. Any overflow of water which is outside this margin is casual water, and you may take relief without penalty.

HOW TO TAKE RELIEF

For casual water **through the green** you find the nearest point which is not nearer the hole, gives relief from the water and is not in a hazard or on a green. Then you drop your ball within one club length of this point.

In a bunker you drop the ball at a spot not nearer the hole which gives relief from the water but is still in the bunker. Relief is not always possible from casual water in bunkers. If the free drop gives you nowhere reasonable to play from within the bunker, you may drop outside, under penalty of 1 stroke. You must keep the point where the ball lay directly between you and the hole.

On the green you lift your ball and place it in the *nearest position* which gives relief and is not nearer the hole or in a hazard. Remember that you must take the nearest position when pools of water lie on the green. Many players move to the line which they think gives the easiest putt, rather than taking the nearest point of relief. You may clean the ball when you lift it.

Bear in mind that you must be on the putting surface to claim relief from casual water which is on your line. If your ball comes to rest just off the green, you must tackle the problem of water between you and the hole without claiming relief.

You may lose a ball in large amounts of casual water. In that case you take relief without penalty, proceeding from the point where your ball passed the margin of the casual water. There must be reasonable evidence that your ball was lost in the water for you to claim relief. Otherwise you treat the ball as lost with the usual penalties.

Ground under repair

Maintenance work needs to be done constantly to keep a course in prime condition. Inevitably you'll meet areas of ground under repair, but take heart – you can claim relief.

Your ball does not necessarily have to be in ground under repair for you to claim relief. If your stance is affected you may also lift and drop your ball in accordance with the rules.

The committee decides what areas of the course are portioned off as ground under repair – usually marked as GUR. Any stakes and lines used to define the area are counted as part of the ground under repair zone.

Material piled up ready for removal and holes made by a greenkeeper are also ground under repair, even when they are not marked as such.

Grass cuttings and other materials which have been left on the course without any intention of removing them – such as fairway

▲ Leaves piled up ready for removal are ground under repair – this area includes the defining line. A sign usually marks the zone.

▼ Bad weather or simple wear and tear can lead to large areas of GUR. If your ball lands here or your stance is affected you can claim relief.

Check for relief
When drainage channels are being constructed they are ground under repair and you can claim relief from them. If the work is fairly extensive the channels might not be marked as such – but don't take relief for granted. Be sure to check the GUR notice in the clubhouse saying you can take a free drop if your ball lands in these areas.

mowings dumped in adjoining woods – are not ground under repair, unless they are labelled GUR.

Remember that with free drops it is your decision whether to play the ball as it lies or drop without penalty. This is important in the case of ground under repair, as you often find that your lie in the GUR area is better than the one you can expect if you lift and drop the ball.

But check the noticeboard in the clubhouse carefully – you can't always choose to play the ball as it lies. The committee has the power to make a local rule, prohibiting play from ground under repair and directing that you must drop a ball away from it.

HOW TO PROCEED

You claim relief almost exactly as you do from casual water or a hole made by a burrowing animal. **Through the green** you find the nearest point of relief which is not in a hazard or on a putting green and not nearer to the hole. You drop within a club length of this.

In a hazard you drop as near as possible to where the ball lay, but not nearer the hole. You must remain in the hazard.

On the green you lift your ball and place it at the nearest point on the green which gives relief from the ground under repair and is not nearer the hole.

Just occasionally you may lose a ball in ground under repair – for example when there are major earthworks on the course to construct a new green or tee. There is no penalty for a ball lost like this – you take relief from the point where the ball crossed the margin of the ground under repair. But there must be reasonable evidence that the ball was lost there and not somewhere else, otherwise the ball is treated as lost.

Questions and answers: Ground under repair

High ball

Q I lost my ball high in a tree in an area marked as ground under repair. Without penalty I dropped a ball a club length from the point where the ball had crossed the line marking the zone. Was this correct?

A The margin of ground under repair does not extend upwards, so you weren't able to claim relief. This was a normal lost ball and you should have proceeded accordingly.

Course cracks

Q During a recent hot summer, wide cracks in the earth appeared in our course. Do the rules of golf provide relief from these?

A No – but the committee would be justified in declaring such cracks to be ground under repair.

Mysterious holes

Q I notice that the definition of ground under repair includes a hole made by a greenkeeper. This seems vague – can you explain it?

A It *is* a vague term to include in the rules. The R and A help a little – their book of decisions states that the term usually applies to ground dug up in connection with course maintenance, such as removing turf and laying pipelines.

Unlucky drop

Q Last week my ball came to rest in ground under repair. The nearest point of relief was in dense bushes – but on the other side of the area was fairway. Surely I should not have dropped in the bushes, where I was worse off? This provided no relief at all. If I was not allowed to drop on the fairway, could I go back and drop behind the GUR area, where there was a decent lie?

A You illustrate a common misunderstanding of this rule. You are permitted relief *only from the particular condition* – in this case ground under repair – in accordance with the procedures laid down in the rules. These clearly state that you must proceed from the nearest point of relief on the course. If this is the bushes, you're merely unlucky – just as you would be lucky to be beside the fairway and allowed a free drop there.

Of course, you could have played the ball as it lay from within the ground under repair. It's your decision, unless the committee makes a local rule stating that you must take relief from the area.

Tree debris

Q Does a tree stump constitute ground under repair?

A No – you could have relief without penalty only if the stump was marked as ground under repair, or was in the process of being dug up or cut up for removal.

Burrowing animals

**If you find your ball in an animal scrape or hole
you may think you can claim
automatic relief, but be careful – the rules about
burrowing animals are quite specific.**

You are allowed relief without penalty from certain types of damage to the course. This includes a hole, a mound of cast soil or the scraped entranceway made by a burrowing mammal, reptile or bird.

When your ball lies in or touches any of these – or if one interferes with your stance or the area of your intended swing – you may take relief without penalty.

You can instead opt to play the ball as it lies if you think you are likely to have a worse lie after lifting and dropping your ball. The choice is normally yours but check local rules – they may insist that you take a drop.

What exactly is a burrowing animal? Pet dogs sometimes dig holes, but the rules of golf exclude them from this classification. Burrowers are those creatures that

make a hole to live or shelter in – such as moles and rabbits. You must have reasonable evidence that a scrape or hole has been made by a burrowing animal – check for telltale signs such as droppings.

The committee can make a hole dug by a dog ground under repair, but that is no comfort to you if you come upon this sort of damage before it's been noticed.

Rabbits are attracted to sandy soils so links and heathland courses are especially likely to suffer from holes and scrapes. Except in a water hazard you can take a free drop if your ball lands in a hole made by a rabbit or other burrowing animal.

CLAIMING RELIEF

The way in which you take relief from damage caused by burrowing animals is almost the same as relief from casual water or ground under repair.

Through the green you find the nearest point of relief which is not closer to the hole and not in a hazard or on a green. Then drop your ball within a club length of this point. If it comes to rest more than a club length from where you dropped it, or if it rolls nearer the hole, you redrop.

In a bunker you drop within the hazard, as near as possible to where the ball lay but not nearer the hole, on a spot which gives you the maximum available relief from the damage. You may instead choose to drop outside the bunker – keeping the point where the ball lay between you and the hole – but this costs you a penalty shot.

There is an important exception to the rule allowing free relief from damage caused by burrowing animals. When a ball lies in or touches a **water hazard** you are not entitled to relief from this sort of damage. You must either play the ball as it lies or drop clear of the hazard under the penalty of 1 stroke.

On the green you are entitled to line of sight relief, even if the damage is some distance from your ball. You lift and place as near as possible to where your ball lay but clear of interference by the damage and not nearer the hole. Bear in mind that if you are just off the green there is no relief from line of sight damage.

▼ **If you find your ball in a rabbit scrape in a bunker you must drop in the hazard to claim relief without penalty. You can opt to drop outside the bunker, but in that case you take a penalty stroke.**

Questions and answers

Which hole?

Q Recently my ball came to rest in a hole which could have been either a divot mark or a hole made by a burrowing animal. After some discussion, I played the ball as it lay to make sure I was within the rules. Could I have lifted it to check whether this was in fact a hole made by a burrowing animal?

A You did the sensible thing. If in doubt always play the ball as it lies. In the case you describe you can lift the ball to check, provided that you tell your fellow player what you are going to do and give him the chance to watch the lifting. If there is evidence that the hole is caused by a burrowing animal you can take relief. If not, you must replace the ball without penalty.

Lucky lie

Q My opponent in a match last week took relief in the rough because his stance was affected by a rabbit scrape. He dropped the ball a club length from the nearest point of relief but not nearer the hole. This gave him a clear view of the green and he could play directly towards it. But from his original lie he had trees in front of him – he would have had to play sideways on to the fairway. Was the relief he claimed permissible?

A Yes, the actions you describe comply with the rules. It is his good fortune if his line of play is improved.

Obstructed ball

Q My opponent's ball was unplayable under a bush. As he prepared to lift and drop under penalty he found the ball was on a mound made by a burrowing animal. He dropped clear of the bush without penalty and was able to play a clear shot. Was this in order?

A A player cannot claim relief if he is unable to play a stroke because of interference by something other than the damage caused by the burrowing animal. In this case, your opponent was unable to play because of the bush.

Newly planted trees

**Sometimes there is a need for a special local rule
to cover circumstances not allowed
for in the rules of golf – such as how to protect
a newly planted tree from damage.**

With so many new courses being built and storm damage needing repair, you are almost certain to come across young trees planted to separate fairways, shape dog-legs or restore natural character to a modified landscape.

Local rules usually protect young trees. The committee has the power to introduce these local regulations, but in doing so they must not override a rule of golf. Always carefully check the wording of local rules on the card of the course, or in the clubhouse in the case of temporary local rules.

The R and A has issued a recommended wording for a local rule to protect young trees. It says that if a young staked tree interferes with your stance or the area of your intended swing, you must lift the ball without penalty and drop it in accordance with the rules.

◀▼ Once you've ascertained that your swing would damage a staked tree, you claim relief without penalty. First mark the position of your ball with a tee peg. Then move back to the nearest spot which gives you a clear swing. Make sure you don't move closer to the hole.

Questions and answers

Seeking protection

Q I am on the committee of my golf club. We have recently planted an area with expensive saplings and wish to protect them. We propose to make a local rule requiring that a player whose ball lies in this area must drop outside it under penalty of 1 stroke. Is this in order?

A No – if you wish to forbid play from an area like this, you may declare it ground under repair and direct that players *must* take relief from it. But you are not allowed to declare a local rule imposing a penalty of a stroke.

Costly error

Q My opponent's ball came to rest within a group of young staked trees. He had a good lie and decided to play the ball as it lay. He did so without any damage to the trees, and went on to make a par on the hole. But I noticed on the card that the local rule for staked trees directed that the ball must be lifted and dropped clear in these circumstances. What is the ruling?

A Your opponent was in breach of the local rule. The fact that he extracted his ball without damaging the trees is irrelevant. In matchplay, he would lose the hole to you. In strokeplay, he would be penalized 2 strokes. If he didn't go back and play from the correct place before striking from the next tee, he would face disqualification.

Committee choice

Q I understand that the committee can define an area containing young trees as ground under repair. Can they direct that players taking relief from the GUR must drop the ball behind the area, so that they keep the trees between them and the hole?

A No, but if the normal ground under repair relief does not seem feasible, the committee could consider establishing dropping zones where balls must be dropped under the local rule.

▲▼ **When you have found the nearest point of relief from a staked tree, mark this new position with a tee peg. Measure one club length from the mark – it makes sense to measure with the longest club in your bag. Standing straight, with your arm held out either to your side or front, drop the ball. Make sure that it lands within one club length.**

You may clean the ball when you lift it.

When taking relief from a staked tree you find the nearest point where the tree does not interfere and is not nearer the hole, and drop within a club length of this point.

Once the trees have matured enough not to need protection, the stakes are removed and the trees must fend for themselves. Golfers are then left to tackle balls which come to rest among the trees as best they can.

CLAIMING RELIEF

Make the most of your advantage but be sure you follow the correct procedure or your luck may turn to disaster. Always check the card and the club noticeboards carefully for the wording involved.

Sometimes, for instance, you will find that you must drop in a dropping zone.

Though the R and A does not like the use of these zones, except as a temporary measure, they are occasionally necessary. For example, the erection of stands and hospitality tents for professional tournaments can make it impossible to play from some areas of the course.

Remember that you probably *must* lift and drop your ball when it lies near young trees, rather than having the choice of lifting or playing the ball as it lies, as is usual with other forms of relief without penalty. Since in this case the committee is trying to protect the young staked trees rather than the golfer, the wording usually directs that you *must* rather than *may* lift your ball.

Glossary

Address
Your position in relation to the ball as you prepare to strike.

Albatross
A score of three under par on a hole.

Alignment
How your body is aligned in relation to an imagined ball-to-target line.

Birdie
A score of one under par on a hole.

Blind
A hole or shot where you can't see your target.

Bogey
Originally the expected score in which a good player was reckoned to complete a hole, but now replaced by par. Bogey has come to mean one over par.

Borrow
How much you have to aim right or left when putting to allow for the slope of the green to bring the ball back to the hole.

Bunker
A natural or artificial depression on a fairway or round the green. It is usually half-filled with sand but can be made of earth or grass.

Chip and run
A low shot that runs towards the flag played from near the green.

Clubface
The area of the club that you use to hit the ball.

Clubhead
The part of the club attached to the lower end of the shaft, and used for striking the ball.

Divot
A chunk of turf removed by the clubhead when you play a shot, usually on the fairway.

Dog-leg
A hole with a fairway that bends sharply. A hazard is often positioned at the angle of the dog-leg to put you off driving across it.

Double bogey
A score of two over par for a hole.

Drive
A shot which is played from the tee, usually with a driver (a 1 wood).

Eagle
A score of two under par on a hole.

Flagstick
Also called the pin, flag or stick, the flagstick marks the hole.

Fourball
A matchplay or strokeplay game of two players on each side, all four striking their own ball.

Foursome
A matchplay or strokeplay game between two sides of two players each, the partners striking the ball alternately.

Full set
The 14 clubs which are allowed for playing a round. A full set usually consists of three or four wooden clubs or metal woods, nine or ten irons and a putter.

Grip
The part of the club you hold, and the way you hold it.

Guttie
A ball made from gutta percha. It lost popularity when the wound ball was introduced at the beginning of the 20th century.

Half set
Either the odd or the even irons, two woods and a putter. A half set of clubs is all you need when you start playing.

Filling in a scorecard
Scorecards are used in strokeplay to record your score so your Club can work out your handicap. As you play a round, you write down the number of strokes taken for each hole and tot up the total at the end. When you have filled in four scorecards, you hand them in and are given a handicap that's your average number of strokes over par.

The par is worked out according to the length of the hole and the stroke index lists the holes in order of difficulty. This is for when you play a matchplay game: if your opponent has a handicap of, say, 10 and yours is 26 you can take 12 extra strokes – three quarters of the difference between your handicaps – on the 12 most difficult holes.

Event MONTHLY MEDAL
Date
STANDARD SCRATCH SCORE 70
Player BILL JOHNSTONE
Handicap FOR H'CAP
Strokes Recd.

Marker's Score	Hole	Yards	PAR	Stroke Index	Player's Score	Won X Lost - Half 0	Marker's Score	Hole	Yards	PAR	Stroke Index	Player's Score	Won x Lost - Half 0
5	1	293	4	13	5								
6	2	356	4	6	5			10	156	3	14	4	3
4	3	169	3	15	4			11	300	4	16	5	4
6	4	454	4	1	7			12	362	4	4	6	5
4	5	301	4	17	6			13	121	3	18	3	4
4	6	305	4	12	4			14	383	4	5	6	6
4	7	335	4	3	4			15	327	4	11	4	5
6	8	396	4	8	7			16	408	4	2	4	5
5	9	365	4	10	5			17	399	4	7	5	6
44	OUT	2974	35		47			18	479	5	9	5	5
								IN	2935	35		42	
								OUT	2974	35		47	
								TOTAL	5909	70		89	

Player's Signature Bill Johnstone
Marker's Signature John Thomson
HANDICAP
NET SCORE
Strokes are taken at those holes opposite which the Stroke Index figure is equal to, or less than, the number of strokes received.

Handicap
A system devised to make play between golfers of different standards an even match. Your handicap is the number of strokes over par you average over four rounds at a golf club. For instance, if your average score is 88 on a par 72 course, you are given a handicap of 16. In strokeplay, if you play with, say, a 2 handicapper, you are allowed 14 – the difference between your handicaps – extra strokes, one on each of the most difficult 14 holes. In matchplay, the longer handicap player would receive 11 shots – three quarters of the difference.

Hazard
A bunker is a hazard. So, too, is any stream, ditch, lake or pond defined as a hazard by a club's committee.

Hole
This can mean either the actual hole that you putt into or the entire area between tee and green.

Iron
Irons are metal-headed clubs used for most shots between tee and green. Sometimes you can use them from the tee at holes where accuracy is more important than length. The sand wedge and pitching wedge are also irons.

Lie
Where the ball is in relation to the ground it is resting on. The more embedded in grass or sand the ball is, the worse the lie. Lie also refers to the angle of the sole of the clubhead to the shaft.

Loft
The angle of the clubface to the ground. The more loft a club has (indicated by how high the number is) the higher the ball goes and the shorter distance it travels.

Long game
Shots over about 180yd (164m) long, played from the tee or on the fairway with woods or low-numbered irons.

Matchplay
A game between two players or two sides which is determined by the number of holes won and lost.

Out of bounds
A ball is out of bounds if it lands anywhere prohibited for play – usually beyond the course's boundaries.

Par
The standard score for a hole, usually based on its length. Holes up to 250yd (228m) long are par 3s, up to 475yd (434m) par 4s and any longer than that are par 5s. Club committees are now authorised to vary par when a hole's difficulty warrants not sticking rigidly to the distances laid down.

Pitch
A reasonably high shot on to the green, travelling anything from a few yards to 120yd (110m). You generally use a 9 iron, a pitching wedge or a sand wedge.

Pitching wedge
A short iron with a large degree of loft, used for pitching high but short shots on to the green.

Play-off
If a competition ends with a tie, the winner is decided by playing further holes. Nowadays, the winner is usually the first competitor to win a hole, except for the US and British Opens.

Reading the green
Looking at the slope and contours of the green to decide the line and speed of your putt.

Rough
Grass left to grow so that off-line shots are made more difficult.

Sand wedge
Also called a sand iron, the shortest, most lofted iron used for playing out of bunkers and for very short pitches.

Scratch player
A golfer with a handicap of zero.

Shaft
The length of the club down to the clubhead.

Short game
Chipping, pitching, bunker play and putting on the green and around it up to a distance of 100yd (90m) away.

Square
When the clubface is placed at right angles to the imaginary ball-to-target line.

Stableford
A popular system of scoring by points for holes completed: par = 2 points; 1 under par = 3 points; 2 under par = 4 points; 1 over par = 1 point.

Stance
The position of your feet just before playing a shot.

Standard scratch score (SSS)
The score expected of a scratch player on any given course.

Strokeplay
A competition in which a player's total strokes for a round are recorded to be compared with the scores of other competitors. 'Strokeplay', the correct term, is often referred to as 'medal play'.

Stymie
A rule now abolished, where a player who was about to putt his ball into the hole, but had another one blocking its route, had to try to putt round or loft his ball over the other.

Swingweight
The weight and balance of a club. All the clubs in your set should be the same swingweight.

Takeaway
The start of the backswing.

Tee
The area of a hole from which you play the first shot.

Tee peg
You can put the ball on this device for your first shot to help raise the ball off the ground. It is then much easier to attain height.

Tempo
The timing and rhythm of your swing, which should be even and smooth throughout.

Thin
A long, low shot hit by mistake with the leading edge of the club (blade).

Top
A shot mistakenly hit with the bottom edge of the club, so that the ball is embedded in the ground before popping up, and in most cases travelling only a short distance.

Triple bogey
A score of three over par on a hole.

Wood
A club normally used for distance shots. It can be made of wood, metal or graphite.

Yardage (distance) chart
A plan of the holes on a course showing the distance from one point to another. It can be printed by the club or prepared by the golfer or his caddie.

Yips
A condition where the player is so anxious about his putting that he can't swing his putter back, and the stroke becomes a jerky jab at the ball.